## ADDITIONAL PRAISE FOR *UNLEASHING THE INNOVATORS*

"Innovation and the ability to challenge the status quo are what ensures the long-term success of any company. The bigger, the more successful the enterprise, the tougher the challenge, and the greater the need. Jim Stengel and *Unleashing the Innovators* offers critical insight into how to evolve a company's culture to constantly innovate, disrupt accepted thinking, and actually benefit from the accelerating change we are all experiencing. Plus, Stengel's lessons will help any individual personally challenge themselves to improve."

—Dawn Hudson, CMO, the National Football League, and Board of Directors, Nvidia and Interpublic Group

"Jim takes us beyond the benefits of partnerships with startups. He forces us to understand two essential human truths critical to innovation—the humility to recognize that no one organization or individual has all the answers and the courage to act on that."

—Salman Amin, COO, SC Johnson

"Jim Stengel aims the invaluable lessons of *Unleashing the Innovators* squarely at the leaders of legacy companies who labor to stay fresh and innovative. Stengel shows how to invite startup innovators into the tent to shock incumbents into new thinking; how outsiders—or insiders who think like renegades—are essential to the longevity of established companies; and a set of 'how tos'—to avoid failure, and to make these unconventional and often uncomfortable partnerships with upstarts work."

—Judy Olian, dean, and John E. Anderson Chair in Management, UCLA Anderson School of Management

"In today's digital, customer-first world, businesses must disrupt or be disrupted. Jim Stengel's fresh perspectives on leadership and purpose are an inspiring call to action for business transformation. *Unleashing the Innovators* is the established company's playbook for how to reignite passion and innovation within corporate culture to survive and thrive."

—Karen Quintos, Chief Customer Officer, Dell

# UNLEASHING THE INNOVATORS

# UNLEASHING THE INNOVATORS

How Mature Companies Find New Life
with Startups

## JIM STENGEL

with Tom Post

CROWN
BUSINESS

**NEW YORK**

Crown Business books are available at special discounts for bulk
purchases for sales promotions or corporate use. Special editions,
including personalized covers, excerpts of existing books, or books with
corporate logos, can be created in large quantities for special needs.
For more information, contact Premium Sales at (212) 572-2232 or
email specialmarkets@penguinrandomhouse.com.

Library of Congress Cataloging-in-Publication data is available upon
request.

ISBN 978-0-451-49723-9
Ebook ISBN 978-0-451-49724-6

Printed in the United States of America

Book design by Lauren Dong
Jacket design by Dan Donohue

10 9 8 7 6 5 4 3 2 1

First Edition

*For my wife, Kathleen,*
*who fosters the innovative spirit in me,*
*our children, Claire and Trevor,*
*and in so many others.*

# CONTENTS

# PLAYBILL

*A List of Major Characters in the Book (in Order of Appearance)*

**Zackery Hicks,** CIO of Toyota Motor North America and CEO of Toyota Connected. Hicks is not just studying human behavior to transform the automobile but also trying to push the limits of mobility into completely new areas with the help of partnerships with startups.

**Tim Armstrong,** CEO of Oath, a Verizon division that includes AOL and Yahoo brands, and former president of Google America's operations. Having served at small and large companies and been on both sides of acquisitions, Armstrong has seen the good, the bad, and the ugly at startups and enterprise companies.

**Steve Ellis,** executive vice president and head of the Innovation Group at Wells Fargo, oversees the bank's partnerships with startups.

**Reese Schroeder,** managing director of Motorola Solutions Venture Capital. Betting on more than two hundred startups over two decades, Schroeder has achieved a great ROI by focusing less on money than on how investments can help Motorola.

**Joanna Seddon,** president of global brand consulting at OgilvyRED. A keen observer of human nature as well as a brilliant researcher, Seddon has overseen the first quantitative study of global partnerships between enterprises and startups.

**Ben Kaufman,** founder and CEO of Quirky, a now-defunct startup that crowdsourced new products and teamed up with GE in a venture that tried to do too much, too fast.

**Beth Comstock,** vice chair of GE, who oversees GE Business Innovations. More entrepreneur than executive, Comstock has helped reinvent the industrial giant by embracing the lean-startup practices of Eric Ries and partnering with dozens of startups.

**David S. Rose,** founder of New York Angels and CEO of Gust, an online platform that connects investors with startups. An entrepreneur since adolescence, Rose believes legacy companies are headed to annihilation unless they enact radical changes.

**Tina Sharkey,** a Bay Area entrepreneur and venture capitalist who has a long history of putting together startups and large enterprises, helping to sort out and reconcile their differences, and putting them on a path to growth.

**Brian Tockman,** principal at 301 INC, the venture group at General Mills, tasked with finding new companies that can vault the old food company into exciting new areas.

**John Haugen,** VP and general manager of 301 INC and Brian Tockman's boss. A long-serving veteran of General Mills, Haugen now spends his time with progressive, young food companies.

**Jeffrey Immelt,** chairman of GE. Although he's held the office since 2001, Immelt has lately behaved much more like an outsider than a long-serving insider. He has spearheaded FastWorks* and given active support to partnerships with startups.

**Viv Goldstein,** global director of innovation acceleration at GE. As cofounder of FastWorks, a multiyear effort to make the industrial giant leaner, faster, and smarter, she has overseen the FastWorks engagement with thousands and thousands of employees.

**Janice Semper,** leader, GE Culture. Few people know the people who work at the digital industrial giant as well as she. An HR specialist,

---

* Trademark of General Electric Company

Semper has been an indispensable player in making GE's epic make-over, FastWorks, meaningful to executives and the rank and file.

**Zain Jaffer,** founder and CEO of Vungle, which inserts highly targeted, entertaining ads into short videos. An immigrant from the United Kingdom, Jaffer has rapidly built a company devoted to serving smartphone addicts and the brands that support the apps.

**Aaron Levie,** cofounder and CEO of Box, which allows users to store, manipulate, and share digital files. Partnering with giants like IBM and Procter & Gamble, Levie has found a new role beyond technical services: helping these companies rethink their processes.

**Sue Siegel,** CEO of GE Ventures and healthymagination. A seasoned venture capitalist and corporate executive, Siegel oversees GE's expanding portfolio of investments and partnerships with startups.

**Braden More,** head of partnerships and industry relations for Wells Fargo's payments business. Reporting to innovation guru Steve Ellis, More created an accelerator that works with just a handful of targeted startups each year.

**Brian Cornell,** CEO of Target. Coming in soon after the failure of the Canadian expansion, the hacking of credit cards, and a slow embrace of the digital age, Cornell has pushed innovative practices and partnerships on many fronts.

**Gene Han,** head of the San Francisco Innovation Center for Target. Arriving in the United States as a boy from South Korea, Han has harnessed his engineering and business smarts to Target's embrace of the Internet of Things. Han oversees its Open House, where walk-ins can try out new gizmos.

**Stephen Gold,** CMO of IBM Watson. Having worked as an entrepreneur, Gold knows what's involved in dealing with startups when they partner with Big Blue's mighty artificial intelligence engine, Watson.

**Ginni Rometty,** CEO of IBM. Rometty has long championed new businesses at IBM and is a strong supporter of Watson, putting big money and resources behind it.

**Paul Steinberg,** chief technology officer at Motorola Solutions. If you want to know what the "first responder of the future" might look like, talk to Steinberg, who oversees Motorola's investments and partnerships with imaginative young companies.

**Eduardo Conrado,** chief innovation and strategy officer at Motorola Solutions. No one has worked more assiduously to keep the company in the forefront of exciting new challenges. Conrado helps settle on Motorola's "hunting grounds"—the areas where it seeks radically new approaches to business challenges.

**Sean Taylor,** senior strategy manager, Motorola Solutions. Part of Reese Schroeder's liaison team, Taylor manages day-to-day doings at startups in partnership with Motorola.

**Scott Jensen,** founder and CEO of Rhythm Superfoods. Can kale and BBQ really coexist? Jensen is at the frontier of new flavors, and he helps General Mills's 301 INC prospect for new partnerships.

**Toby Rush,** founder and CEO of EyeVerify, a biometric and security startup that partnered with Wells Fargo before being acquired by the Chinese e-commerce giant Alibaba.

**Arthur Tisi,** cofounder and CEO at Connectidy. A musician by love and training, Tisi is teaming up with IBM Watson for an "emotionally intelligent" online dating service.

**Naomi Kelman,** founder and CEO of Willow. A veteran healthcare executive, Kelman has produced a radically different kind of breast pump that's quiet, can be tucked into a bra, and is easily cleaned in a dishwasher.

**Ryan Broshar,** a managing director at Techstars. He is overseeing an accelerator program for Target in Minneapolis.

**Kristin Nielson,** director of innovation at Target. She oversees the Techstars accelerator program from the Target side.

**Carlos Moncayo Castillo** (along with brothers **Luis** and **Fernando**), cofounders of Inspectorio, a global supply chain platform providing real-time information to retailers and brands. Carlos is a Techstars alum now partnering with Target.

**Jacqueline Ros,** CEO and cofounder of Revolar, which produces a wearable alert system that helps women ward off assaults. Ros is another alum of the Target Techstars.

**Don White,** cofounder of Satisfi Labs, a mobile shopping assistant that is partnering with IBM Watson to enrich the brick-and-mortar experience in chains such as Macy's.

**Deborah Kilpatrick,** CEO of Evidation Health, a startup hatched by Stanford Health Care and GE Ventures that quantifies product impact in the digital era of medicine.

**Alex Hertel,** cofounder and CEO of Xperiel, which helps sports franchises such as the Sacramento Kings and New York Jets enrich fan engagement via an easily programmed platform that connects digital devices, from smartphones and Jumbotrons to team apps and cash registers.

**Jesse Robbins,** founder of Orion Labs. Its main offering is Onyx, a smart walkie-talkie that has grabbed the attention of Motorola Solutions.

**James "J.C." Curleigh,** executive vice president at Levi Strauss & Co. and president of the Levi's brand, helped kick off the denim maker's Jacquard partnership after a chance encounter with a Google executive.

**Chip Bergh,** president and CEO, Levi Strauss & Co. A twenty-eight-year veteran of Procter & Gamble, Bergh arrived at the old denim maker in 2011 to shake things up and jump-start sales. He opened the

Eureka Innovation Lab and exhorted his team to test new limits for apparel with unlikely partners.

**Ivan Poupyrev,** technical program lead at Google's Advanced Technology and Projects Lab, an in-house tech incubator. The Russian-born computer scientist worked at Sony and Disney before joining Google. Among other things, he oversees Jacquard, a partnership with Levi's that produced the "smart" Commuter jacket.

**Bart Sights,** senior director for technical innovation at Levi Strauss. Sights grew up in his family denim business. Now he's testing all kinds of new fabrics and held up the Levi's side of the Jacquard partnership with Google.

**Paul Dillinger,** head of global product innovation at Levi Strauss. As Bart Sights's colleague, Dillinger was the point guy on Jacquard and has witnessed all the highs and lows of the partnership.

**Karyn Hillman,** chief product officer at Levi Strauss.

**Kris Tulin-Roberts,** senior director of innovation at Levi Strauss.

**Stacy Flynn** and **Christopher Stanev,** cofounders of Evrnu, a startup that is developing fabric from 100 percent recycled cotton, using 80 percent less energy. Evrnu and Levi's have been working on a partnership.

**Will Papa,** chief R&D officer, The Hershey Co. Another Procter & Gamble alumnus, Papa is leading the storied chocolatier into new artisanal confections and healthy snacks, often by partnering with startups. His work has inured him to the likelihood of having far more failures than breakthroughs.

**David Kidder,** cofounder and CEO of Bionic, a New York firm whose Growth OS helps create a startup ecosystem within large enterprises, delivering the methods and tools of lean entrepreneurship and the portfolio outlook of venture capitalists. His work inside GE is helping to drive its reinvention.

**Aarif Aziz,** HR leader for India, ASEAN, and Africa at GE Healthcare. Aziz instituted the DARE Award, which recognizes failed efforts and encourages employees to discuss and share stories of near misses.

**Rick Dalzell,** former CIO of Walmart and then of Amazon, where he promoted the Just Do It Award, which highlighted well-intentioned, independent projects that never succeeded but pushed employees to keep trying new things.

**Danielle Weisberg** and **Carly Zakin,** cofounders of theSkimm, which shoots a free online newsletter to millions of subscribers.

**Rick Morrison,** cofounder and CEO of Comprehend Systems, a platform that helps Big Pharma monitor, analyze, and share data from multiple clinical trials, patient enrollments, and compliance information.

**John Phelan,** practice leader, and **Sarah Plantenberg,** senior designer, IBM Bluemix Garage, San Francisco. This duo leads a dynamic consultancy that deals with outside clients and stirs up processes and products within IBM itself.

**Flemming Ørnskov,** CEO of Shire, a biotechnology company that specializes in rare diseases. A Danish-born physician, Ørnskov has more than doubled sales by partnering with startups of various sizes, some of which he's acquired.

**Durk Jager,** former CEO of Procter & Gamble. A dynamic and creative leader, Jager aggressively drove changes throughout P&G in the 1990s.

**Greg Brown,** CEO of Motorola Solutions. Brown has embraced the ideas and approaches of outsiders, from shareholder activists like Carl Icahn to promising startups from the United States and Israel. He says his biggest takeaway over the last decade is becoming a better listener.

**Kevin Colleran,** managing director of Slow Ventures, a venture capital firm. As an early employee at Facebook, Colleran was instrumental in overseeing partnerships with giants such as P&G.

# UNLEASHING
# THE
# INNOVATORS

# Introduction

We let the outside in, and that helped unleash our innovators in-house.

—Zackery Hicks, *chief information officer of Toyota Motor North America and CEO of Toyota Connected*

I DID NOT GO INTO THIS BOOK PROJECT LOOKING TO WRITE A playbook for culture change and growth for established enterprises. I was simply curious WHY so many existing companies and startups were working together. As a former global head of marketing at a major organization, I wanted to know WHAT was really going on with these odd couples. I was sure there would be some interesting lessons and stories in those matchups.

What I discovered—in our two years of intensive interviews and in our large-scale global study conducted by OglivyRED—is that established companies that partner with startups, and successfully scale those lessons across their broad company culture, are winning at renewing themselves and reinvigorating innovation and growth.

It seems that every executive, and every company, is struggling today with the pace of change, looking for new ways to grow their enterprise. By bringing together the old and the new, the experienced wisdom of an established firm with the energy and speed of the entrepreneurial, companies are able to bring fresh blood and new ways of doing things into their organizations. And startups are able to learn how to scale up more quickly and establish new channels more effectively. Done right, it is a win-win for both. This book is a playbook for solving that essential equation.

In our global study, we found that enterprises with successful startup partnerships are THREE TIMES more likely to have a major positive impact on their entire organization than those with unsuccessful partnerships.

In a sense, we have discovered the corporate Fountain of Youth—and it is located not among the mangroves and sawgrass of Florida, but in the workings of successful partnerships between iconic companies and energetic startups.

Are you struggling to change your company culture? Are you looking for a new approach to grow your business? Maybe it's time to unleash the innovators inside your own organization. In the next pages, you'll see how other companies are successfully tackling the challenge.

# 1

# What Keeps Companies Up at Night

We're not always the smartest people in the world.

—STEVE ELLIS, *head of the Innovation Group at Wells Fargo*

THE IDEA FOR THIS BOOK BEGAN PERCOLATING A DECADE AGO. A couple of years before I left Procter & Gamble in 2008 as its global marketing officer, I was attending Google Zeitgeist, the annual thought leadership event at the tech giant's headquarters in Mountain View, California. I was there with other Fortune 500 company leaders, the kinds of people Google was courting to experiment with its search capabilities and its newly acquired video platform, YouTube.

On an unusually warm September evening in Silicon Valley, I had a revelation while dining under the stars with Google founders Sergey Brin and Larry Page. I already knew that this brash and growing technology giant would lean heavily on companies such as P&G. Of course it would: Google, or Alphabet, as it is now known, is able to poke into all those potentially life-altering innovations—from self-driving cars to balloon-powered Internet access—only by selling lots and lots of ads. So, obviously, it needed large advertisers. My cross-current thought was that we at P&G couldn't survive without Google, as well as an exaltation of startups bent on changing the world. And that was probably true of other large, mature companies.

Why did we need startups? Not just because they offered indispensable products and services to P&G—but because they did business in a radically different way. They were engines of continual creativity; they engaged passionately with their audiences and customers; they hired the best and the brightest people, people who loved working there. In fact, they were sparking a dangerous talent drain away from mature companies like ours. They didn't have to poach skilled, smart young people because the choice between working for an established company and an exciting upstart with endless potential to become the next Facebook or Uber was really no choice at all.

*Exuberance. Passion. Excitement. Audacity. Intensity.* These were the words I would use to describe Google and companies like it. These were also things I hadn't felt as intensely at P&G for many years.

Upstarts such as Google in its early days reminded me of what life must have been like in the earliest days at the biggest and oldest corporations. Every venerable established company— P&G, IBM, Levi Strauss, Target, Toyota, Wells Fargo, GE, Motorola Solutions—started with a dynamic founder, a brilliant idea, and a determination to deliver something extraordinary and transformative. But as companies grow—acquiring more customers, developing more products and services, bringing on more investors and strategic partners—those companies lose their original excitement, purpose, and drive as the years grind by. They become more concerned about how to maintain market share or survive in their space than about how to transform the world. In a word, they go from bold to *old*.

If we at P&G, a 170-year-old company at the time, didn't start to learn from these companies and adopt their agility and speed—retrofitting our own operations to restore some of the charisma and fast-paced performance of startups—we would lose relevance with our employees and with consumers. *Is this fossilization among mature companies reversible?* I wondered.

On the flight back to Cincinnati, I started to scratch out a plan to learn from these new companies whose energy was garnering so much attention. Step one was to reconnect with Tim Armstrong, president of Google's Americas operation, and invite his group to P&G's headquarters in Cincinnati. (Since 2009 Tim has been CEO of AOL, now part of Oath, a division of Verizon.) Could our very different teams and cultures push beyond the ad-selling commercial relationship?

Imagine my excitement when, a few weeks after my visit to Google, Armstrong and his Google team descended on Cincinnati. We agreed that the best way to mix with and fully understand each other's culture was to do a brief employee exchange. We sent leaders from a few of our largest brands, including Tide, to work at Google for a month. And Tim dispatched Google people to work in the daily rituals and rhythms of brand management at P&G. Both sides wrote up what they had learned and presented it broadly within each organization. (The *Wall Street Journal* got wind of the idea and put the story on its front page in November 2008.)

What did Procter get out of it? Google got us to loosen up a bit during a spoof campaign of Tide to Go, a stain-removing pen, and gave us a taste of user-generated content. Tim's Google squad also persuaded us to wade ankle-deep into online marketing by empowering so-called mommy bloggers to write about Pampers.

And what did Google get out of it? Google learned that a big, established company like P&G could teach them a few things about brand management. As we taught Tim how P&G worked with leading retailers such as Walmart and Target, he came to realize that the sales organization he'd built at Google didn't work for big clients. Why not set Google up along the lines that P&G had—focused on dominant customers and categories, instead of on geography?

But the fun didn't last. That innovative experiment was never repeated. Not long afterward, I retired from P&G after twenty-five years and started my own business, The Jim Stengel Company, helping enterprises large and small work through challenges of activating their brand's purpose, developing their organizational culture, and renewing brand strategy and positioning. Still, those stimulating weeks of Google/P&G cross-pollination have never been far from my mind.

Over the last nine years, as I've dealt with scores of clients, given hundreds of talks, and had meetings with countless executives, I've sensed a growing anxiety—sometimes bordering on panic—throughout the business community. Why? Increasing global competition has had a hand in it. So has rapidly evolving technology, along with the tilt of resources and media attention to anything digital. The Great Recession was a punishing gut punch, delivering a fatal blow to some businesses. There's residual angst. Everyone worries constantly about survival, about who or what's around the corner, about how they're going to deal with it, outlive it, prosper again.

Let's be blunt: many legacy companies are in trouble because their brands don't mean as much to consumers anymore. Women really don't obsess about Tide's latest line extension. Budweiser and its new stepbrother, Miller, are no longer the top choices of millennials, who probably live or work near a craft brewpub that makes more innovative beer. In a world of Tesla and Uber, who identifies as much with Chevy and Ford anymore? Older brands need to acknowledge that the world has changed—and start acting more like startups. And not just try to buy them, the way GM put the moves on Lyft.

And startups can learn something valuable from legacy companies as well. Most startups need a little parental supervision. Failure rates for young companies are abysmally high. They often lack discipline, structure, the ability to scale up without losing their core culture or mission—in short, the wisdom of an experienced organization. Some young entrepreneur superstars could use a dose of corporate humility. It might forestall their sudden fall. We've all seen more than a few unicorns, those upstarts supposedly worth $1 billion or more, turn into donkeys.

Companies—large and small, old and young—don't need to go it alone anymore. They're beginning to interact with each other, establishing powerful new kinds of alliances. Those that don't, that struggle on their own, repeating the same bad habits, are gambling with their future. Unsuccessful startups will die off quickly. Older businesses, larded with resources but continuing their traditional ways of doing business, risk suffering a protracted, painful death.

In my work as an executive at P&G and later as an entrepreneur, I began to see that the distinct species of startups and legacy companies actually share a lot of the same DNA. By working together, they can learn a great deal from each other. The impossible energy and drive of a startup company can help rejuvenate an established firm, injecting some of its mojo, innovation, agility, and commitment.

Startups can teach older companies how to move faster, take more risks, learn from failure. On the flipside, established companies have much to offer startups in terms of growth, distribution, capability development, and longevity. They can teach startups how to create a brand that fosters a lasting emotional bond; how to build an organization to support global expansion; how to deal with multiple constituents, from board members and shareholders to giant corporate customers and joint ventures. Bridging the different worlds of young and old may turn out to be key to surviving in a swiftly changing and increasingly complex and dynamic world.

Few leaders from established companies would disagree. This book is designed primarily for them, for the executives and managers and aspiring managers of legacy companies who realize their organizations have grown sclerotic, defensive, and less responsive to their constituents, and who feel an urgent imperative to change. The key question for them is: *How?*

Cross-pollinations, like the brief embrace of P&G and Google back in 2008, are taking place at forward-looking enterprises. Motorola Solutions, for example, the public safety technology company created in 2011 when Motorola split in two, is partnering with a gaggle of startups on ventures that sometimes sync with its strategic focus but are often outside its orbit of expertise. It recently started the process to set up an incubator in Israel to stay abreast of the latest tech trends.

GE has been teaming up with new companies to transform its 125-year-old company into a lean and mean machine to bring products to market faster. At Wells Fargo, established 165 years ago, an accelerator culls dynamic young financial technology companies, in groups of three twice a year, and teases out products that push the bank out to the frontiers of greater financial security and better customer service. "We're smart enough to know that we're not always the smartest people in the world," says Steve Ellis, who oversees the bank's Innovation Group. "Some of the best ideas come from startups."

None of those ideas can take root, much less flourish, without unqualified support from the CEO. "I really do think a lot of it starts at the top of an organization and flows down through the staff," says Reese Schroeder, the executive who runs the venture capital arm of Motorola Solutions. I heard a version of that truism every time I talked to a legacy company engaged in partnerships with startups. And not just a drive-by blessing of these efforts, but a shoulder-to-the-wheel, get-your-hands-dirty engagement in the work, cheering on the efforts and galvanizing the entire company around the idea of innovation and change. Involvement by the C-suite is such a strong theme—along with humility, learning, planning for success, and embracing experimentation—that leadership is the subject of Chapter 10.

In this book I will examine some of these partnerships, showcasing how aging established enterprises are gaining new strength and relearning old skills from the most imaginative and innovative up-and-comers, learning to sweep clean even the darkest, most cobwebbed corners of the organization with the stiffest of brushes. It will serve as a practical guide for legacy companies considering such partnerships, showing what works, what doesn't, and why—a playbook brought to life through storytelling.

To buttress these conclusions I commissioned what we call the Global Partnership Study, a first-of-its-kind global study of 201 established companies and startups from OgilvyRED, a research-based consultancy. It adds quantitative underpinnings to a qualitative investigation (my team and I traveled to fifteen cities to interview more than one hundred leaders of fifty legacy companies and startups). Leading the OgilvyRED group was Joanna Seddon, Ogilvy's president of global brand consulting, whom I first worked with when she made a gripping presentation in 2007 to our senior management at P&G, challenging many of the ways we did business. I admired her keen intellect—Joanna has a BA, an MA, and a doctorate from Oxford—and her chops as an entrepreneur, having launched consultancies within FutureBrand and Millward Brown (a part of WPP) and founded the BrandZ Top 100 Global Brands annual study. She saw around the corner that research was moving from data dumps to sharp analytics that made sense of all the information—and she knew how to build great teams. So I tapped her talents again in 2011 to help me with my first book, *Grow*, while studying the link between brand purpose and financial value creation. This time around, she is laying an important foundation for the storytelling, helping to pinpoint the opportunities and chokepoints of these new partnerships, as well as emerging trends. You'll see references to the Global Partnership Study throughout the book.

Collaborations can be tough, and sometimes downright frustrating, for both parties. More than a few of them end in divorce. Consider, for example, the mixed record of GE, which has done as much as any major corporation to shake itself up in order to become a more nimble giant, more sensitive to what its customers want and need.

One of its notable partnerships started as a love affair. But it ended up in divorce court. In 2013, GE partnered with Quirky, a startup with a novel platform for developing consumer products on an ultra-fast track. GE wanted to coproduce some new appliances, like smart air conditioners and Wi-Fi-enabled lightbulbs. But it also wanted mightily to rejuvenate itself, and hoped Quirky and its founder, Ben Kaufman, could help its people and its culture learn to take more risks, live with failure, and generate new products that it could get to market a lot quicker. In essence, it wanted to rediscover its youth. "Ben is just fearless," Beth Comstock, the vice chair of GE and the president and CEO of GE Business Innovations, told me. "He trained some of our guys to just think faster and figure it out as you're going forward." But she also had her doubts. "It may end up being a black eye for GE that we backed something that's not going to work."

Six months later, Quirky was bankrupt. Customers were furious at the lack of support for the products the two companies had introduced. Forced to step in and deal with those complaints, GE had a few of its own. Quirky's collapse, it charged in court papers, "caused substantial damage to the reputation of GE and to its trademark." Not just a black eye—a complete orbital blowout.

Still, GE Ventures, the company's innovation and disruption arm, isn't giving up on startups. It is backing dozens and dozens of new ventures in such areas as energy, healthcare, advanced manufacturing, and software. One of them, Airware, is a drone technology company that built an operating system integrating the many different software systems that run unmanned aerial vehicles with the cloud, analyzing, storing, and distributing the data. GE is collaborating with Airware to send out drones that can monitor power lines, oil pipelines, and wind turbines—with the hope of transforming the services it provides to customers, increasing safety, and reducing downtime. To date, GE is thrilled with the venture.

So why did one effort to rediscover innovation flop, while another flourished? What journeys of self-discovery are legacy companies taking? How are they reaching for something outside themselves in order to find their way home again?

For the answers, read on.

# 2

# Can Mature Companies Avoid Self-Destruction?

*We needed to go outside ourselves to be reminded that we
actually had capacity within ourselves all along.*

—BETH COMSTOCK, *vice chair, General Electric*

O N A CRISP FEBRUARY MORNING IN NEW YORK CITY'S CHEL-
sea neighborhood, David S. Rose is doing what he loves
most: evangelizing about startups. Picture singer-songwriter
John Denver about five years older, a bit heavier, with rim-
less glasses, and you've got his physical aspect about right. But
there's nothing 1970s mellow about Rose, an entrepreneur and
investor who is now running Gust, a giant platform he created
to match early-stage startups with investors. He takes his verses
from "The End of the World as We Know It," not "Sunshine on
My Shoulder"—at least when it comes to talking about startups'
antithesis: big, old established companies.

In Rose's philosophy, founders are hero-creators whose paradigm shifts rock the planet—mostly for the good of humankind.
Enterprises have largely outlived their usefulness and just get in
the way of those young creators unless they're toppled by them.
It sounds like something I remember from my Greek mythol-
ogy course at Franklin & Marshall College.

"Startups begin with an entrepreneur who sees something
no one else does," says Rose, whose long startup career began
at age twelve when he decided to manage his younger broth-

er's magic shows. "The entrepreneur creates something from a standing start, taking account of the world as it exists, with no preconceived notions. Large corporations are the opposite." By contrast, they operate "not in the world as it exists at that point, but at points at which the business *has* been operational . . . the essence of creation happened in the past, and the present world rarely factors in."

None of that sounds particularly depressing until Rose starts a long exposition of economic theory. He launches into the Industrial Revolution, then sweeps in Joseph Schumpeter's theory of creative destruction (constantly revolutionizing economic structures from within), later twentieth-century capitalist cataclysms brought on by the digital age and other dislocations, and the need to "solve some end problem unbounded by preconceived anything."

His view of commercial history isn't just bleakly Darwinian; it verges on an ode to anarchy. The most successful businesses, Rose argues, don't just overturn whole industries, as Steve Jobs did with personal computing, then the music business and camera manufacturers. They routinely, deliberately blow *themselves* up.

Jeff Bezos disrupted Len Riggio's dominant Barnes & Noble bookstore chain by offering a wider selection of books online. After revolutionizing the book industry, he upended retailing by forming partnerships with other manufacturers and selling everything from clothes to cameras online, quickly challenging big box stores like Best Buy and Walmart, and becoming the Everything Store. Next he asked himself, "Who will do to me what I did to him?" in the bookstore space. So he upstaged his own paranoia by introducing the electronic reading device, the Kindle. Next, Bezos worried about how a competitor such as Netflix would draw a bead on distributing digital movies and TV shows, and so created streaming services via Amazon

Video. After that, he realized that the entire game was in the cloud and—boom—he created Amazon Web Services, which stole an early lead on Google, Apple, and Microsoft. Next he created a sweeping transformation of the logistics business (as in local sourcing and drones). All because of Bezos's insistence on wiping the slate clean again and again. Rose neatly summarizes: "Bezos says, 'I don't care what constraints exist; I'm going to start totally from scratch.' " It's enough to make a lot of corporate heads gyrate.

"Business is so fundamentally changed every day in every way," Rose continues, "that you have to be aware of everything *outside* your space. Your safe, convenient world is gone forever." Business, he goes on, "is not flat, nor is it a staircase or an escalator or even a high-speed elevator. It's a frigging rocket ship, and you always have to look forward or you'll be left behind."

What's a résumé-heavy, struggling executive in the Fortune 500 supposed to do?

"Any company designed for success in the twentieth century is doomed to failure in the twenty-first century," Rose assures my coauthor, Tom Post, and me. "Unless your company develops the ability to think and act like an entrepreneur, you're doomed! Blow up your own bridge and start with no preconceptions." An hour, at least, has passed in the bleak and windowless conference room with only a white board for adornment. Rose remembers he has another appointment and stops the interview abruptly. As I head out the door, he offers one more piece of advice. "Change can't be incremental," he says. "There has to be a genetic level of change—something insane, exponential!"

Outside, the wind slicing along 28th Street seems to carry an extra bite. *Is this guy for real?* If Rose's thesis is true, do established companies have a prayer of thriving again?

## RISK AVERSION: THE OPIATE OF THE CORPORATE MASSES

Over the next several months, I interviewed dozens of startup founders, venture capitalists, angel investors, and, especially, corporate chieftains. And Rose's extreme views began to take on a commonplace character. What he says is undeniable: Legacy companies are in trouble, and they know it. They've snuffed their own spark through their own long-term success, as well as by adding layers and lawyers, and all the programs and procedures they've codified and cantilevered to perpetuate that success.

Most established enterprises haven't invented anything truly dynamic in decades. Procter & Gamble, the perennial most-admired company (and my alma mater), has produced no transformational new brands since Swiffer and Febreze back in the early 2000s, although they have strengthened core brands with initiatives like Tide PODS, Gillette Fusion, and Pampers Swaddlers.

As in many mature companies, P&G's people are more preoccupied with their career progression as P&G's top-line growth has slowed. Promotions are few and far between. Leaders are drawn to the safe, the sure, the proven, the known. Blow themselves up? Many are afraid the tiniest failed experiment could stall their career. At the same time, they know deep in their bones that something has to give.

Among all the established enterprise companies you'll meet in this book, there is something akin to entrepreneurial envy. They covet the speed, scrappiness, vision, flexibility, and—let's face it—"cool" factor of the best startups, the ultimate magnet for new talent. They realize they need to somehow capture it, reclaim a long-lost knack, without giving up everything that's core to their business. In other words, imagine if Procter & Gamble had an amazing water-free technology to get clothes clean: how would they commercialize it without sacrificing Tide, Downy, or Bounce? It reminds me a little of older friends who wish they were young again but also want to hold on to their years of experience ("If I knew then what I know now . . ."). The hope is that by bottling some form of entrepreneurship, a mature company can rejuvenate itself.

## GAINING MOJO VIA MERGERS: IT DOESN'T WORK

The classic way to seize the startup spirit is to acquire it. Seeking to shake up its own e-commerce business, Walmart, sturdy if not lithe at fifty-four years old, bought Jet.com, an Amazon-like retailer founded in 2014, for an anything-but-discounted $3.3 billion. The 160-year-old General Mills spent an undisclosed sum to take a stake in another young startup: two-year-old Epic Provisions, which combines organic meats such as bison and uncured bacon with snack bars and trail mix—concoctions perhaps once thought too bizarre for the food chemists in Minneapolis, the hometown of General Mills.

The idea: buy a needed technology or a toehold in a burgeoning market. It happens all the time among "aging" tech companies (Microsoft's purchase of LinkedIn; Google's grab of Nest; Apple's purchase of Beats Electronics), newish tech giants (Facebook's acquisitions of WhatsApp and Instagram), and Fortune 500 companies ogling mature and declining tech companies (Verizon snatching up Yahoo).

But most mergers and acquisitions are unsuccessful. Far from acquiring those elusive synergies or getting a revenue shot in the arm, acquiring companies tend to fare poorly compared with industry rivals in such key areas as profit margins, earnings growth, return on capital, and share price. So says an August 2016 study by S&P Global Market Intelligence, which analyzed the Russell 3000 (an index of the three thousand largest publicly held companies in the United States) back to 2001. In a classic 2011 *Harvard Business Review* article, Clayton Christensen and colleagues clocked the M&A failure rate at between 70 percent and 90 percent. An acquisition has, in other words, about the same chance of survival as a startup.

BabyCenter, an infant commerce startup headed for bankruptcy, nearly died a second time after it was picked up by Johnson & Johnson in 2001. They bought it "for a song; it was like a marketing spend," recalls Tina Sharkey, a San Francisco entrepreneur and venture capitalist. "But they didn't know what they'd bought." A cofounder of iVillage, an early online media site for women, and former CEO of Sherpa Foundry, which helps public companies identify new sources of innovation and growth, Sharkey was called in to fix the deal. J&J, she says, had unreasonable financial expectations for BabyCenter from day one. "I said there's not a snowball's chance I can hit the numbers," says Sharkey, a rapid talker who adapts an incongruously relaxed-looking yoga pose while sitting in one of her red hollowegg-shaped chairs.

Sharkey's first order of business was to partner with P&G, partly to convince J&J insiders to pay attention and in part to distance BabyCenter from its new owner. "I had to tell the trade press we were not beholden to J&J. We had to change focus and engage with new and expecting moms," she remembers. Within months, she had to acquire another property, a social media platform devoted to young mothers, in order to set her "toddler" in the right direction. Over time, BabyCenter became a global destination site. But what a lot of effort, much of it spent straightening out the acquirer.

## PARTNERSHIPS: WHY THEY'RE REPLACING TRADITIONAL ACQUISITIONS

A lot of executives at established companies I've talked to are now treating acquisitions more as a last resort. The bolt-on acquisition is very old-school. When it comes to dealing with startups, the new paradigm is partnerships.

Put differently, the old archetype is about getting married: acquire a company until death—or divorce—splits you asunder. The new model is about having affairs: fool around with partners—a lot of them—in order to suit your different needs. Why settle on one relationship when you can have many of them?

But for what purpose? Almost as many reasons as there are companies that engage in them. To acquire expertise in a particular area, for sure. Very often to add to a line of core businesses. But a surprising number of these companies use partnerships with startups in order to fish in new waters and see what the tides kick up. More remarkable still, the most forward-leaning legacy corporations are trying to remake themselves from within, relying on young companies to teach and reteach some basic lessons in how to innovate better, take risks again, reach decisions without painful complexity, develop new products and services more quickly, and recapture enough flair to draw the best and the brightest—both new hires and new customers—to the company.

Unlike an acquisition, which is little different from an organ transplant, these sundry partnerships act in the best cases like a miraculous immunotherapy drug: a powerful kick to the body's T cells so that they can fight the aging disease from within.

The why of partnerships is the subject of Chapter 3. But it's worth headlining a few of the reasons corporations choose to engage with startups. Two-thirds of the mature companies surveyed in our Global Partnership Study say they partner in order to foster innovation, followed by solving a particular problem (64 percent), leveraging a startup's tech savvy (54 percent), and bringing new products to market faster (52 percent). Down near the bottom of the list of motivations is something I'll be talking about a lot in this book: changing the corporate culture to make it more entrepreneurial and risk-taking (35 percent). Very often older companies initially get involved with startups for specific reasons that may change and deepen over the course of the relationship.

These partnerships take many forms. At their simplest, they embody a commercial relationship, like the one between Procter & Gamble and Box, a cloud-based startup for simple, secure file sharing and collaboration. Some are straight-up venture-capital-like investments in startups; that's typical of General Mills. Others offer entrepreneur-in-residence programs, traditionally the role of venture capital firms.

Still others, such as Wells Fargo, create incubators or accelerators for young companies. The boldest among the legacy companies engage in homegrown experiments, suggestive of smaller-scale Google X "moon shots," but with the aim of actually making money. Those inside-the-company efforts have roots going back seventy-plus years to Lockheed's Skunk Works, which produced such memorable designs as the XP-80, an airframe to accommodate the most powerful jet engine in World War II, and the U-2 spy plane. (Skunk Works still exists today, sometimes working with competitors such as Boeing, whose Phantom Works grew out of R&D at McDonnell Douglas.) A few companies, such as Target, Wells Fargo, IBM, and General Electric, engage in more than one kind of partnership, and do so simultaneously.

## INTRAPRENEURSHIP WITH A NEW TWIST: A MEANS TO REVIVE THE ENTIRE COMPANY

Intrapreneurs—entrepreneurs within a large firm—were once a hot topic in business academics, as well as at companies that gave long leashes to creative individuals. Intrapreneurs created some fabled products: Post-it notes (3M), personal/desktop computing and the computer mouse (developed by Xerox but commercialized by other companies), and the four-bit central processing unit (Intel). More recently, giants such as Virgin (Media, Mobile, Air) and Microsoft (Xbox) have found success by letting their most creative people run with some wild ideas that turned into popular and profitable products and services.

But despite widespread experimentation, the classic intrapreneurship of the 1980s, 1990s, and 2000s faltered more often than not. As with many failed acquisitions, the problems mainly resulted from the rejection of an organ transplant: the organizational body proved hostile to a foreign enterprise, eventually killing it.

As far back as 1984, Gifford Pinchot III warned of corporate hostility to these crazy visionary types within the company (*Intrapreneuring: Why You Don't Have to Leave the Corporation to Become an Entrepreneur*), calling the phenomenon the "corporate immune system." Bureaucracy, hierarchy, rules as rigid as commandments, punishment for failure—all these things would conspire to strangle too many young vines before they climbed. Pinchot proved prescient in all but his title. It turned out that for the most part you *did* have to leave the company to become an entrepreneur.

Today's intrapreneurship probably needs a new term because it's a different incarnation, no longer the idea of the past. In the few places where it's taking root—in companies such as GE and, in earlier stages, Target, Motorola Solutions, IBM, and Wells

Fargo—it involves a transplantation of something new and different inside a corporation that is itself undergoing irrevocable and sometimes radical change. Instead of parceling out a tiny garden patch for new growth among the vast acres of vintage produce, the current champions of intrapreneurship are preparing all their soil and scattering new seeds throughout the stronger and more established crops.

And here's something that caught me by surprise. The most evolved mature companies are starting to treat a startup partner as an agent of their *own* deep-channeled commitment to change, not just as a portfolio company investment or an opportunity for technology transfer. We discovered this in our dozens of onsite interviews with executives of mature companies, and found it affirmed in our study with OgilvyRED: companies with successful partnerships were three times more likely to have a major positive impact on their organization. That alone is reason enough to double down on your startup partnership efforts.

## A CASE STUDY IN CONTRASTS

There's probably no better illustration of this experience than a comparison of the efforts of General Mills and General Electric, each wrestling with the gargantuan labors of transforming themselves. Legendary companies both, they are at different points on the continuum when it comes to scaling the lessons of entrepreneurs across the enterprise.

On a late July morning, over coffee with Brian Tockman and John Haugen, I heard about General Mills's attempts at revitalization. Downtown is already hot enough to melt license plates, but inside the Starbucks in the Loews Minneapolis Hotel you can almost feel comfortable in your skin. These guys are pathfinders to innovations in food, and head up its fledgling venture capital practice.

Haugen, who arrived fifteen minutes late returning from a fishing trip with his kids, is in his early fifties with a full head of gray hair, two days of beard growth, and engaging blue eyes—the classic good looks of a Jon Huntsman Jr., the former governor of Utah. A twenty-five-year veteran of General Mills, he's the boss of 301 INC, the team tasked with reinvigorating the $17 billion (in sales) food company. He came up through marketing, new-product development, and health and wellness initiatives. Tockman, with closely cropped brown hair, is boyish-looking and bespectacled. He had an earlier stint at General Mills as a financial analyst but detoured into startup life for a handful of years before his return in 2013. Haugen pulls up a chair, leans forward, and does most of the talking.

Created in 2012, 301 INC started out as a new-product incubator for General Mills. But after launching eight new food products—one of them Nibblr, a snack-by-subscription service—the enterprise "hit a brick wall." What happened? "We concluded we couldn't 'out-entrepreneur' what was happening in the marketplace," says Haugen. More soberly, they realized the company was not creating new businesses at the pace it needed. "It's not that you can't find ideas; it's that you don't let enough great ideas in." To be sure, it's hard to think of a true blowout category General Mills invented—not something it acquired or bought into with another company—since Hamburger Helper, which was first introduced in 1971, or Nature Valley granola bars in 1975 (though Haugen does mention the company's leadership in products like Go-Gurt, or Yoplait in a tube, and in bringing whole grains to many cereals).

What accounts for this kind of protracted dry spell? Haugen, who has spent half his life at General Mills, ticks off the usual reasons that innovation falters, ones that I have heard over and over again at large, mature corporations:

- The wrong people are put in charge of innovation.
- The right people parachute in, but they never have a chance to produce something great because, like everyone else, they're constantly rotated in and out of divisions.
- Both time and investment are insufficient.
- There are "sandbox" issues, where the venture is too isolated from everything else at the company.
- There's a lack of authentic stories of trial, error, and success to help kindle excitement throughout the organization.
- The corporate sword of Damocles—aka the constant threat of spending cuts—discourages innovation.

## SMALL INVESTMENTS, BABY STEPS

So 301 INC morphed into a venture group. Now led by a team of fifteen, it rapidly invested in a handful of startups, including Epic Provisions (which it bought), Good Culture (an organic, high-protein redo of cottage cheese), and Rhythm Superfoods (kale chips, beet chips, and other "nutrient-dense" snacks). Recently it added to its portfolio D's Naturals (plant-based performance products), Farmhouse Culture (probiotic foods and drinks), and Purely Elizabeth (ancient grain granola, oatmeal, muesli).

"We want to be an indispensable partner to these companies," Haugen says. General Mills helps them with developing their sales channels, creating consistency in product quality, and building marketing and branding strategies, as well as strong overall operations. Often General Mills brings the new brands into their internal store, giving employees a chance to sample the new wares. At the same time, says Haugen, "I firmly believe this"—investing in startups—"is an important strategic tool to identify future growth for General Mills."

This is toe-dipping into unknown waters, for sure. But aside from testing potential new product extensions, General Mills is enabling some bilateral learning when it brings these startups into the organization. Higher-ups start to understand what it is about their corporate climate that drives startups nuts—and sometimes out the door: the "black-hole" syndrome into which so many ideas disappear; the glacial pace when it comes to getting anything done; the fact that contacts, to say nothing of champions, constantly change and you never know whom you're going to be dealing with next; and that executives can sometimes behave with incomprehensible arrogance. General Mills employees—especially millennials—get a boost, too. The more they get wind of what's going on at 301 INC, the more likely they are to believe the company has ongoing relevance and staying power in the future.

301 INC is starting to get attention within General Mills. The night before meeting Haugen and Tockman I had dinner with a trio of midlevel executives at the company, people in their mid-thirties, who were aware of the venture but weren't familiar with its details.

A pretty lithe group, 301 INC operates with an internal committee of a half-dozen people who discuss key areas for investment. There's a range of capital to deploy each year; the ante amount flexes to the shape of the idea and the scope of opportunity. Every investment still needs approval from the top. "I do this within the company balance sheet; we're not a standalone," says Haugen. He believes his team brings other benefits to the organization at large. A broad selection of General Mills folks can participate in biweekly "sample days," to review products sent by startups and send back their unvarnished opinions. Overall, Haugen believes 301 INC "helps protect the company's flank" by investing in brands that align with and might possibly bring new areas of growth to existing brands.

How does Haugen scout for these prospects? You'll hear more about him and 301 INC in Chapter 4, where we explore both systematic and more chancy approaches.

As we part company after our hour-and-a-half sit-down, I have to ask Haugen: What's with the 301 INC name? It turns out it honors the address of the original flour mill of General Mills, which began as the Minneapolis Milling Company in 1866. Nice. Respectful. Heritage is important. The tagline for 301 INC—"the Emerging Brand Elevator"—is reminiscent of the ubiquitous grain elevators in the Midwest. The challenge of course is to leverage the power of their rich heritage while at the same time challenging it.

## A LEAN, MEAN REJUVENATION MACHINE

We're now going to explore what's been going on simultaneously at GE, where its large-scale reinvention is a few years ahead of General Mills.

The changes at GE are neatly embodied in a massive, companywide movement called FastWorks,* already in its fifth incarnation. The term embodies both a rough-and-tumble declarative goal, with an emphasis on speed, and a nod to its past—as in Edison Machine Works, a predecessor company to GE dedicated to electric motors and dynamos. The company has been moving away from its earlier history as rapidly as an organization with 170,000-plus salaried employees and numerous multibillion-dollar businesses can. It has jettisoned its real-estate portfolio, its appliance unit, and its finance arm. And it recently decamped from its pastoral headquarters in

---

\* Trademark of General Electric Company

Fairfield, Connecticut, to set up in gritty, tech-happy Boston, in a twelve-story glass building that connects two old brick warehouses. The design by the architectural firm Gensler, which will be completed in 2018, is meant to marry history with the future.

All this signals a profound transformation of purpose. Long-serving CEO Jeffrey Immelt has said that GE will become one of the world's leading software companies by 2020. That was laughable back in 2011, when he first went public with that ambition. Today, with a focus sharpened toward industrial businesses—aircraft engines, locomotives, power generators, oil and gas equipment, medical imaging—and cloud-based applications to make them run smarter and more efficiently, that goal isn't so laughable anymore.

Along with this colossal realignment, GE Ventures has been partnering with one hundred or so startups, some working on products of strategic importance that are clearly in sync with its business, others engaged in helping the corporation rediscover agility and velocity. "I know from the partnerships we've had, we're relearning the ability to be fast," says Beth Comstock, the company's vice chair, who oversees GE Business Innovations and has spearheaded FastWorks. "When you're a startup, you don't have a lot of resources, so you have to make decisions quickly—and based on what you have on hand."

The multi-fronted efforts began in early 2011 with the hiring of William Ruh, a recruit from Cisco Systems, who took a $1 billion grubstake and set up a software subsidiary in San Ramon, California, to develop an operating system for GE's industrial operations. That was its first big flag planted in Silicon Valley. Things quickly kicked into higher gear. That fall, Comstock attended a signing of Eric Ries's new book, *The Lean Startup*, and told Immelt about its premise: that successful entrepreneurs quickly produce a minimum viable product (MVP)

and Southeast Asian markets, where neonatal deaths occur at an appalling rate, often from hypothermia.

To create an MVP (minimally viable product), the group inverted its usual method of development by canvassing its customers—in this case, midwives and nurses—about what they needed, instead of creating something in Chicago (or, now, the United Kingdom, where GE Healthcare is based) and foisting it on in-country salespeople. The device had to accommodate itself to poor, rural communities with periodic power blackouts; be easy to use for caregivers with minimal training; and tolerate extreme changes in voltage and humidity. It also had to be relatively inexpensive ($1,200), with low maintenance and repair costs. GE has sold a couple of thousand units.

## KILL THE ANNUAL REVIEW

In FastWorks 3.0, a 2015 project, Semper and Goldstein began kneading the corporate culture, folding the initiative into every aspect of the company's systems and giving folks an action plan. They started remaking its performance management system, relying on constant coaching and feedback, instead of annual reviews, to get everyone reading from the same script as far as GE's resculpted vision goes. "We've even experimented with doing away with ratings," confides Goldstein. For a few seconds, an awed hush falls on the conference room where we're gathered. And based on the experiment, lessons, and positive response from participants in the pilot program, Susan Peters, senior vice president for HR at GE, announced globally in July 2016 that the company would no longer give annual static ratings to its employees.

Perhaps down the road they'll start compensating people differently—for trying and failing, instead of meeting prescribed benchmarks. "We're still trying to figure out how incentives can encourage risk-taking," says Semper. "We are testing the ability to say, 'Here's your reward: Go spend it in the way that's most meaningful to you.'"

## EVEN INNOVATION NEEDS A RESET

In 2016, FastWorks began the year by tackling the arduous process of organic growth, a critical test of how well the new commandments, imported from the outside, are taking hold. Midway through the year, though, GE had to reboot. "There was some confusion among employees," explains Goldstein. "FastWorks isn't prescriptive. We decided that it didn't *have* to mean the same thing to everybody, that you could take what you want from it and grow with it." The overarching goal "is to create the right solution for customers." Far better if everyone tries to figure out "how to get a better product to market faster." This was an important lesson for Goldstein. The process of rejuvenation is ongoing: "it doesn't have an endpoint." She adds, "Nothing is smooth. Everything is ridiculously hard." Pause. "You have to continually change or you die." Those are words that could just as easily have come from the fervent apostle of startups, David Rose.

So the answer to the question of what legacy companies are getting from partnerships with startups is that they are getting eyes on important new trends, tickets to the future, insurance that they won't be left behind in the next big development, and, most important, catalysts for a clean sweep within in order to make themselves more inventive, more decisive, and more responsive to customers.

## BENEFITS TO STARTUPS: FAR BEYOND FUNDING

And what do startups want to get out of the arrangement? The Global Partnership Study I commissioned actually tracked pretty closely with my interviews with dozens of young companies. Access to general resources and expertise (including mentors) ranked first at 23 percent, followed by funding (21 percent), increased revenue (20 percent), and access to markets and customers (15 percent). Gaining credibility came in at only 11 percent, which is surprising. But slice that last category more finely, and two-thirds of surveyed startups tell you that dealing with legacy companies taught them new ways of thinking and of working. And, in the best cases, greater clarity of purpose and mission.

That's been among the benefits to Vungle, a San Francisco startup that provides hypertargeted, interactive video ads it embeds into mobile games and thousands of apps. Its goal is to give clients a credible, verifiable use of their advertising dollars, serving up consumers who will transact some kind of business, whether it's signing up for something or handing over funds. Put another way, Vungle's aim is to bury John Wanamaker's aphorism—"Half the money I spend on advertising is wasted; the trouble is, I don't know which half"—and establish a new archetype.

"Ads suck because the user experience is awful," says Vungle cofounder Zain Jaffer, twenty-nine. An ethnic Indian, he speaks with a clipped, London-inflected accent, and at the time of our conversation had taken to dyeing his black hair blue after losing a bet that Vungle would notch lower revenue than it actually did. The punk look is by no means a sign of frivolity. Jaffer came up the hard way, demonstrating not just perseverance but jauntiness and cunning as well. "Entrepreneurs with a vision will do anything to realize that vision," he says.

His parents lived in Uganda during Idi Amin's reign of

terror in the 1970s, and were forced to flee to the United Kingdom. "We didn't grow up in a good neighborhood," Jaffer recalls, citing the west London towns of Hayes and Harlington. "A lot of my friends didn't make it," he says without elaboration. At age fifteen, he started tinkering with the Internet, and after he became one of Google's top publishers, he was approached to test its video ad technology. "The experience was awful," he says. "You were lucky if the site loaded and didn't crash your browser."

The first in his family to go to college (he attended Kings College London and also University College London for his master's), Jaffer nearly got kicked out after a raucous party in his flat that drew security and finger-wagging warnings from the school. By then he was on his sixth startup, Mediaroots Ltd., which created video tutorials online—how to use Microsoft Word or Photoshop, for example. One of the cofounders, it turned out, was embezzling, and Jaffer and his other partner had to file an injunction against him. Working and sleeping in his London office, living off discounted meals from British grocery chain, Tesco, that were about to reach their sell-by date, "I lost contact with my family and my friends," Jaffer says. Out of that hardship emerged the idea for Vungle. But the young company was starved for cash.

Jaffer read about a contest sponsored by AngelPad, a startup incubator cofounded by Thomas Korte, who had been a Google international product marketing manager. AngelPad was offering $120,000 for the best startup idea. Since American entrepreneurs seemed to have an inside track, how could Jaffer and cofounder Jack Smith draw attention to themselves from across the pond? They videotaped themselves talking about Vungle, created the headline "Do you know Thomas Korte?," and shelled out the last of their funds to pitch a landing page on ad networks that linked back to the video. That created a lot of buzz and queries to Korte, who found it more annoying than amusing. "He said, 'Take the video down, you got my attention,'" Jaffer recalls. Vungle also bagged the prize, a promising seed round that led to more than $25 million raised in just over two years. By 2017, Vungle achieved a $300 million annual run rate in sales.

But there have been growing pains. Getting traction with customers proved difficult at first. Especially after Apple changed the rules for developers in 2014, essentially prohibiting their apps from displaying shares of social ads that rewarded people for sharing them. These types of ads were an integral part of Vungle's business and its customers relied heavily on them to generate revenue. The restriction was a blow to both Vungle and the mobile app economy, so Jaffer rallied his team to reverse it.

Jaffer met with Vungle's top clients and ad partners to organize an informal coalition to call for a change. The movement stuck and was joined by a chorus of other like-minded mobile companies that also voiced their concerns. Less than a month later, Apple overturned the restriction and Vungle was back on track.

## SURPRISING LESSONS FROM THE MASTERS

Working with clients like Walt Disney Co. and Microsoft, Vungle has refined its mission, making it a far better company. "Our vision has evolved," says Jaffer, a year after my first sit-down with him at his office in San Francisco's South of Market neighborhood on a still rough-and-tumble block. How has it changed? "Sometimes intuition overrules data. But as we get bigger, it's more about data," he explains. By that he means more testing of different versions of video ads with consumers and jumping on so-called event data (the actions users actually take) from advertisers. His clients demand and deserve an ROI on their advertising dollars. "Why should they pay for a click or a view whose KPI [key performance indicator] doesn't matter?" Jaffer asks.

Hoping to deliver more tangible value to its customers, Vungle has moved from cost per view and cost per thousand viewer clicks to KPIs and ROAS (return on advertising spending). If not the holy grail, ROAS at least offers a metric that gets advertisers a step closer to the promised land: a much sharper reading of exactly how mobile users are responding to particular ads, and the long-term ROI of those actions. Its partnerships helped push Vungle in a new and better direction.

"We're now able to quantify every aspect of our lives," says Jaffer. His new model, he thinks, can even help an industry challenged to the point of paralysis: traditional retailers. In a climate where Macy's is struggling to survive and is continually closing stores, Vungle is now working with mobile-first commerce apps to encourage consumers to redeem coupons and ramp up spending.

Again, it's useful to turn to the Global Partnership Study. Better than nine in ten startups that participated in the survey said their partnership gave them credibility; 85 percent cited increased growth; 78 percent mentioned a gain in self-confidence; nearly two-thirds claimed they learned new ways of thinking and working.

## AND A SURPRISING CONTRIBUTION FROM STARTUPS

For Aaron Levie, the CEO and cofounder of Box, a cloud platform to store and share massive documents, partnerships with corporate giants can offer a startup a viable route to fast growth. Companies are budgeting $300 billion a year for software systems of all kinds, he says, so why treat it as a zero-sum game? "If you believe that $300 billion is going to $500 billion and the way to grow that is by developing best-in-class experiences even on your competitors' platforms, now all of a sudden I'm thinking differently—about openness, about collaboration around partnerships," says Levie, who is partnering with old standbys like IBM, Apple, and Microsoft. "You have to believe that you're in a space that is either growing or changing so rapidly that working together gets you to the other side faster."

And Levie cites another reason to traffic with legacy companies. "We would like to be seen more as an outsized partner in their overall transformation strategy," he explains, "whether it's them calling us first when they have a major technology idea, or even if it has nothing to do with our domain, so we can help them navigate that." In other words, to be seen and utilized as a willing agent for change within the corporate partner. You'll hear more about that in Chapter 5, when we meet Levie again.

So you can see what each side gets out of such partnerships. Their benefits should surprise no one: they're the skills and strengths that help every company—of any size, of any age— survive and prosper. The rub is in getting to those goals. "I know *what* the lessons of partnerships are," a senior retail executive told me not long ago. "What I want to learn is the *how*"— the struggle and the means. And those lie at the heart of this book.

# 3

---

# Why Form a Partnership?

It's like Red Bull for innovation.

—Eduardo Conrado, *chief innovation and strategy officer,*
*Motorola Solutions*

O KAY, YOU'VE DECIDED TO FORM A PARTNERSHIP WITH A
startup or two—or ten. The key question to ask yourself is,
how will it serve your needs? And which startup is the ideal
partner?

It's important from the outset to be clear about your goals,
purpose, and expectations. These may shift slightly or even
change radically at any point during the lifetime of an alliance.
But having a clear goal from the get-go ensures a better outcome for both you and the startup.

A lot can go wrong in these relationships. But the number
one cause of frustration among large corporations that have engaged in such partnerships is unmatched or unrealistic expectations. According to the global study OgilvyRED conducted
for us, surveying 100 legacy companies and 101 startups, a
distant second when it comes to causes of frustration is lack
of communication or disconnect, followed by irreconcilable
differences in corporate culture. Lining up those issues at the
start is key.

So, how do you come up with durable rules of engagement?

This chapter is devoted to motivation—to deciding what you

and your company hope to get out of an alliance with a startup, and to set some goals to help ensure a good outcome.

Again, our Global Partnership Study is instructive. Four in ten mature enterprises say their chief goal in partnerships is to increase revenue. Startups, by the way, cite access to resources and expertise (23 percent), getting funding (21 percent), and driving sales (20 percent) as their top motivators.

**GOALS FOR PARTNERSHIPS**

| What Motivates Mature Companies | | What Motivates Startups | |
|---|---|---|---|
| Revenues | 40% | Access to general resources/expertise | 23% |
| Add a new product or service line | 39% | To get funding | 21% |
| Find new approaches to problems | 36% | To drive sales/revenue | 20% |
| Timeframes | 33% | Access to customers/markets | 15% |
| Acquire technology | 31% | Access to distribution/new markets | 13% |
| The number of innovations | 25% | To gain scale | 12% |
| Cultural change | 18% | To leverage (brand) power/gain credibility | 11% |
| Other | 18% | To raise our profile/gain exposure | 10% |
| | | To access technology resources and know-how | 10% |
| | | To leverage marketing skills/channels | 7% |
| | | Other | 22% |

Yet, as you'll see from reading about various established companies that are putting themselves through this experience, there is no prescribed rationale for a partnership or right way of creating rules. General Electric adheres to a set of guiding principles derived from FastWorks, its internal efforts at rejuvenation, which works well for the company. Wells Fargo tries to sync its collaborations with particular business units that have specific objectives.

At IBM, Watson (its artificial intelligence platform) is creating the most exciting business opportunity for Big Blue in a generation—and it's spawning all kinds of new relationships with young companies. Target, like Wells Fargo, has selected a handful of commercial themes to pursue, all focused on growing its core business. As for Motorola Solutions? The folks there have been at the partnership business for two decades and have perhaps the most thoughtful and well-articulated environment for innovation of any ninety-year-old company.

A couple of common themes emerge. Whatever their different approaches, these legacy companies have a sure sense of why they're choosing to ally themselves with startups: they have problems to solve, they want to explore new lines of business in particular areas where they feel they lack experience, and in many cases they're trying to revitalize or reinvent themselves with the help of young companies. It all starts with motivation.

## CALIBRATE EXPECTATIONS TO THE MATURITY OF THE STARTUP

Sue Siegel has a five-point checklist she rigorously applies to GE's partnerships and investments, approximately 30 percent of them with early-stage companies, the rest later-stage. The CEO of GE Ventures and healthymagination, which manages a portfolio of one hundred or so startups, Siegel spent five years as a partner at Mohr Davidow Ventures in Menlo Park, California, before coming to GE in 2012. An even longer history with startups gives her a pretty fair grasp of entrepreneurial success—and the detours that lead to disaster. Those hands-on experiences inform her view of partnerships. Her approach:

- "First, you have to understand your own guidelines. What are you trying to get to? Can this startup provide it? If you go in not knowing the most important thing, you end up asking for everything, and that limits the possibilities for the startup."
- "Second, the startup must win, too. Without that, you don't have a strategic partnership."
- "Third, the startup has to be able to survive as a stand-alone company, an operating company on its own—or you end up supporting it."
- "Fourth, you have to match the stage of the startup to your need. The corporation takes a technical risk—getting to a Series A round—knowing that up front. It's imperative to understand the time horizon to get the outcome the company wants."
- "Fifth, consider the cultural elements. Folks on the corporate side have ten other jobs besides managing the partnership; the startup has one job—to become successful. Matching the stage and the culture and the outcome for each partnership is critical."

Okay. So what *are* you trying to get to?

Here again, it's instructive to see what the Global Partnership Study discovered. Most enterprise organizations focus on very particular objectives. The chief goal for them is increasing revenue (40 percent), followed by adding a new product or service (39 percent), finding new approaches to problems (36 percent), acquiring speed to market (33 percent), and acquiring new technology (31 percent). Cultural change limped in last at 18 percent. Don't be fooled by this; as we have already seen, those who have successful partnerships see dramatic culture change—more on this in Chapter 9. Establishing clear, discrete objectives is the first jumping-off place to secure a good outcome.

But is that alone enough?

Not for legacy companies on a transformational journey. GE is militantly focused on outcomes, but only those that push forward its five core beliefs—what you might call its "holy quintinity." They're concise enough to cite:

1. Customers determine our success.
2. Stay lean and go fast.
3. Learn and adapt to win.
4. Empower and inspire each other.
5. Deliver results in an uncertain world.

### ASK: WHAT'S IN IT FOR THE CUSTOMER—AND A PARTICULAR BUSINESS UNIT?

Wells Fargo hasn't etched its commandments in granite the way GE has. For one thing, the bank isn't trying to make itself over, as the industrial giant is. So Wells Fargo is taking relatively small bites of the fruit of innovation, and doing so in a highly centralized way. A startup accelerator formed in August 2014 invests in and works with just six startups a year: three in the spring and another trio in the fall. And these discrete efforts are guided by the Innovation Group, headed up by Steve Ellis, a revered disruption guru within the bank, who used to oversee wholesale services. "When we think of our accelerator, we have big topics," says Ellis. "Security, customer experience, data analytics." In line with those interests, Wells gravitates to young companies working on such important areas as payments and biometrics, augmented reality, and authentication and fraud.

Braden More, who ran the startup accelerator program until 2017, encourages what he calls "innovation flow" from startups.

But he adds, "We're really only making an investment when we have a commitment from one of our lines of business that shows interest in collaborating with that company." One example: Eye-Verify, a biometric security startup in Kansas City, Missouri, which piqued interest from the Treasury Management Group. "We'd been looking at biometrics since 2008," says More, who started out at Wells Fargo in 2000 as a strategy manager. Dressed in slacks and a polo shirt, he looks as though he'd be more at home on a boat in San Francisco's harbor, thirty-three floors below his office, than in a financial institution.

But at first glimpse, biometrics didn't look all that promising for the bank's purposes. Most startups were exploring voice technology, which is at best 98 percent accurate—an unacceptable success rate for a bank. By contrast, EyeVerify reads blood vessels in the eye's sclera, a signature unique to each individual, and racks up scores that approach 100 percent accuracy.

More contends that a six-month sojourn in the accelerator is long enough to prove or refute a concept and its usefulness to one of the bank's business units, in terms of "making the people that work here more successful for their customers." Now, he says, "we're in the process of deploying EyeVerify to our commercial customers. I believe we'll be the first commercial bank to deploy this kind of technology broadly."

## CHALLENGE PARTNERS TO REIGNITE YOUR INNOVATION DNA

Target's partnerships tend to be tightly tethered to particular areas, too. Throughout its history, Target has been at the vanguard of innovative retail. That innovation has always come from within, and in every era it was born out of necessity.

In the 1920s, Target's founding family, whose initial business was downtown department stores, beat a freight handlers' strike by using airplanes to carry goods from New York to

Minneapolis. And with a stroke of marketing showmanship, they paraded the planes through the streets of the city. The goods they carried sold out right away. As department store operators, they responded to suburban migration during the 1950s by opening the nation's first indoor mall (Minnesota's cold winters can seem relentless).

Target jumped into mass retail in 1962, the same year as then regional players Walmart and Kmart. As Sam Walton's stores grew and laid claim to low-price leadership, Target decided on a different game altogether, becoming an arbiter for "cheap chic." Its playbook for design collaborations and for limited-time-only collections—including those from Michael Graves (with his iconic spin on the tea kettle), Isaac Mizrahi, Missoni, and Lilly Pulitzer—has since been co-opted by plenty of retailers. And today, although much of Target's innovation is still homegrown, it's bringing in outsiders to lift up and accelerate transformation at its core.

Brian Cornell is the first CEO in Target's fifty-five-year-history to come from outside the company. A thirty-year industry veteran, longtime PepsiCo executive, and former CEO of Sam's Club, Safeway, and Michael's, he joined Target on the heels of a disastrous data breach, with clear eyes. He readily admits the company lost its way during the digital revolution, showing up ten years too late.

Cornell confronted some bleak challenges. By 2014, Target's revenue had essentially flatlined. Its first international expansion into Canada looked like a money-loser over the next decade. In short order, Cornell pulled the plug on Canada, sold off Target's middling pharmacy business to CVS, and put a plan together to reshape Target that hewed to its longtime brand equities—style, kids, and families. He also jump-started an initiative to build smaller-format stores in dense urban markets, where more and more of Target's millennial customers were choosing to live but where its traditional stores didn't fit.

Cornell also made changes at the top. Generalists, who once suited the company's long-standing corporate management philosophy, would no longer do. Target needed more specialized expertise. So he brought in seasoned leaders from Amazon and Tesco to transform the company's massive global supply chain. He hired Nordstrom's brand chief to replace legacy brands, representing more than $10 billion worth of goods, with more than a dozen new exclusive brands; all of this happened in less than two years. Cornell challenged his buyers "not to mistake good performance for great potential."

But Target also needed a leadership infusion of a different kind. Up until this time, managers had learned to solve big, complicated problems by bringing to bear the kind of resources a massive corporation could muster. But in an era of unprecedented digital disruption, Cornell needed more entrepreneurs, people willing to take more risks and build programs at a much quicker pace. For the first time, Target was willing to partner with startups, creating a retail accelerator with Techstars, which helps young companies get a start by pairing them with corporate mentors.

Resorting to this sort of outside-in approach is really nothing new to the giant retailer. Target, Cornell reminds me, was created in 1962 in the basement of Dayton's, the department store chain founded in 1902, the same company that developed the first indoor shopping mall. "We were born out of experimentation," he says. "So it's truly part of our DNA."

Target is trying a variety of new approaches and tinkering with them as they go. In June 2015 it created Open House, near San Francisco's Yerba Buena Center for the Arts, a 3,500-square-foot Lucite "home"—part lab, part retail space—

that's loaded with connected electronic gizmos such as smart thermostats, security devices, speakers, appliances, and so on. The idea is less to sell stuff than to learn about how consumers react to the products and the phenomenon of the Internet of Things (answer: it's not a completely warm embrace, at least not yet).

Open House also sponsors meet-ups with local entrepreneurs. Gene Han, who is the head of Target's San Francisco Innovation Center and VP of Consumer Internet of Things, is already rethinking Open House.

You'll read in the next chapter about Target's inaugural venture with Techstars, a mentor-packed accelerator for startups. Working with eleven young companies, Target has sent its own executives to mingle with and coach the founders, making selective investments and partnerships with a few of them.

## LET A MACHINE-DIRECTED AGENDA—AND A THOUSAND STARTUPS—BLOOM

Big Blue claims entrepreneurial chromosomes, too. "IBM has had to reinvent itself several times throughout history," says Stephen Gold, who is CMO of the Watson Group, as well as vice president of partner programs and venture capital investments, at IBM. "And in doing so, it did what many would think would be more aligned to a startup mentality—bet it all." *Mm-hmm, right*, you're tempted to say. Until Gold brings up a couple of radical paradigm shifts from IBM's past: the System 360, the IBM mainframe introduced in the mid-1960s, and e-Business, transactional services built on the relatively new Internet in the mid-1990s.

In 2015, he continues, IBM chairman and CEO Ginni Rometty "stood up at a Gartner industry event and said, 'We believe this is all about a new era of cognitive business.'" Once known as artificial intelligence—a futuristic technology long on promise and scant on delivery, where machines mimic the human brain and people and computers become BFFs (best friends forever)— cognitive computing sweeps in its path natural-language processing, reasoning, machine learning, speech and visual recognition, and a whole lot more. At IBM, cognitive computing has become a potent strategic lodestar known as Watson. Gold calls it the "grand challenge."

Watson can claim that title because it has moved far beyond its splashy triumph against a couple of stellar (and humanoid) *Jeopardy!* winners back in 2011. These days, it's a honey pot for startups and universities, open to any third party. "With Watson, we said from day one we're going to make the very technology we have developed and are using to advance toward meaningful solutions accessible to everyone and anyone," says Gold, who bears a fleeting resemblance to a younger Bob Woodward (of *Washington Post* fame) and speaks with vowels as wide open as the prairie. "You enter the realm of what we call the ecosystem, but it's the world at large."

And it's a world filled with huge possibilities, allowing any individual to mine the planet's data and resolve all that unstructured information into something relevant and meaningful. "This is about making us better as individuals," says Gold. "It's about enhancing, scaling, and accelerating our personal expertise." Watson's genius, if the term can be applied to a technology platform, is that once it's programmed by people, it can learn, understand, and reason on its own. Since its launch in early 2013, the IBM Watson Group has partnered with dozens and dozens of startups and organizations—some paying licensees, others not—for projects big and small.

Some partnerships could be literally lifesaving ventures, like

Watson's alliance with Memorial Sloan Kettering Cancer Center, Quest Diagnostics, the Mayo Clinic, and Pfizer, to hasten more evidence-based care and cancer discoveries.

Others are sheer fun—and potentially quite profitable. WayBlazer, a startup from Terry Jones, who cofounded Travelocity and Kayak, uses Watson to put the travel agent (and personal concierge) back in travel. Macy's recently teamed up with Watson partner Satisfi Labs to create an in-store mobile shopping assistant that's a lot more helpful than many flesh-and-blood salespeople (you'll hear more about this young company, along with a dating app that uses Watson's Tone Analyzer to detect emotions, later on).

IBM has partnered with the chic crowd—helping fashion entrepreneur Georgina Chapman produce a dress that incorporates light-emitting diodes. IBM mingles with the tech and entertainment pack at Austin's yearly South by Southwest Interactive Festival. I dropped by the IBM installation at the 2017 Festival, and through Watson-enabled virtual-reality software I created a virtual world using only my voice. But the highlight was my interview with Watson about my personality type: Watson determined I was a "Mentor" and made me a custom T-shirt on the spot. This is not the IBM I interviewed with coming out of business school in the 1980s.

And it's no surprise that IBM also traffics with the ultra-geek crowd: a troupe of former IBM Watsonites founded CognitiveScale, which is wrestling with the massive problem of the high failure rate of Big Data. "CognitiveScale is a catalyst for us," Gold says. "It's pushing us."

And that's the whole point: to assemble thousands and thousands of entrepreneurs in loose affiliations to discover and push ever-new applications of Watson. "It's proved to be a huge accelerant to these businesses," says Gold. "And I think it's going to redefine what startups, individuals, and developers expect from their partners." IBM is serious about Watson's grand challenge as it expects Watson to reach one billion consumers in 2017.

Artificial intelligence is becoming more infused into many IBM product and service offerings. "When you look at how the technology is actually advancing within the organization itself," Gold explains, "the core capabilities are starting to appear throughout our entire portfolio." It's a pretty smart strategy—use your new business to find new collaborators, and let the resulting partnerships spark and spread change throughout your company.

So far we've seen variations on a couple of game plans, which all start with a clear sense of what these older companies want to achieve in partnerships. Some approaches, like those of GE and Wells Fargo, adhere to pretty strict precepts that pervade the entire company. Others, like Target's and IBM's strategies, begin with a discrete goal but rely on a looser structure governed, perhaps, by a greater willingness to experiment on unknown outcomes.

## CREATE A SMALL HUB WITH MANY SPOKES

Motorola Solutions has been at this longer than most old companies. As a result, it has thought longer and harder about the use of partnerships—and has developed a highly integrated use of these relationships throughout the organization, with active involvement by executives over many years. Its goals for innovation form a small but powerful hub that extends through many spokes. That wheel—more of a flywheel, actually—drives the company forward.

Much of this work seems to happen without much attention from Wall Street or the press. Motorola Solutions was one of two companies formed after the mother company split apart in 2011 (Google got the other half, Motorola Mobility, the handset business and intellectual-property patents for Android; Google sold the mobile device business to Lenovo two years later).

Motorola Solutions provides critical technology to firefighting, law enforcement, and emergency services, as well as to utilities, transportation, and healthcare organizations. That may sound dull, but Motorola Solutions has moved well beyond two-way radios. In fact, it's up to some very cool stuff, including a future concept known as Robocop 2—what chief technology officer Paul Steinberg calls "the connected first responder of the future."

I saw flickers of innovative brilliance firsthand when I served on the board of Motorola from 2005 until the breakup. Those were trying years for the company, overshadowed by Carl Icahn's seemingly endless proxy battles as he tried to gain seats on the board and force the spinoff of Motorola Mobility. In 2012, Motorola Solutions repurchased Icahn's stock for $1.2 billion. Now untethered, the company can finally go its own way.

## PROVIDE A UNIFYING THEME (OR FIVE) TO GUIDE INNOVATION: THE "HUNTING GROUNDS"

Motorola Solutions is slimmer now—its revenue is about 70 percent of what it was during Icahn's involvement—but it is running a lot smarter, with much higher operating and net profit margins. Surely some of that is the result of its innovation ecosystem, a term I hesitate to apply to most companies. But Motorola Solutions has created a true biosphere for new ideas and partnerships. And it starts with a central set of ideas. Unsexy as safety and security may seem, they provide a very ready focus for all sorts of experiments, some of them to help solve a specific problem, others to transform corporate behavior toward innovation, still others to bet on serendipitous outcomes.

"We have 'hunting grounds,'" says Eduardo Conrado, the

chief strategy and innovation officer, "four or five areas that we think are of interest for innovation." Those hunting grounds and their shifting themes attract a lot of trappers and shooters, including Motorola Solutions' own venture capital group, which invests in startups and later-stage young companies; top executives, who constitute a very active investment board; the product strategy team; and an innovation center in Israel.

"There's no monopoly on good ideas," opines Conrado, a twenty-five-year veteran with the courtliness of a European diplomat. He routinely sits down with entrepreneurs in and around Chicago, where Motorola Solutions recently moved, as well as in New York, Silicon Valley, Toronto, and Tel Aviv. "We come back so energized from the visits—it's like Red Bull for innovation. But you also come back a little bit humbled because you go, 'All right, we could be doing this a little faster, a little bit differently.'"

And what do startup partners gain? An infusion of maybe $4 million or $5 million (sometimes more) and a lot of guidance for success. "We bring their technology into a vertical"—that is, offer their products to a specific industry or segment—"or provide a route to market for them," says Conrado.

Everything starts with a consensus on what themes or goals should inhabit the hunting grounds. "Envision a document that has three rows," says Reese Schroeder, the managing director of Motorola Solutions Venture Capital, which has made more than two hundred investments in the past couple of decades. "The bottom row is gaps to fill—we need apps in our portfolio, we need a better battery or a better display, that sort of thing." Next up is "capability enhancement: we need, for example, to enhance our design capabilities. So go out and find some good design companies that we can partner with." The last "is to drive it to strategic themes. There's three of them today: one of them is intelligence-led public safety; one of them is the 'intelligent edge'"—meaning processing data close to the place where it's collected in order to make key decisions—"and the third is the mobile app ecosystem." And there are layers within these layers. "Inside those themes, there are bullet points—and this is what you talk to venture capitalists about because that's how you communicate what you're interested in." In other words, get the word out to your network, which activates the deal flow and shoots back possible candidates.

## SEEK QUARRY IN THE HUNTING GROUNDS

The mobile app ecosystem is one of Motorola Solutions' three strategic areas of focus. This led Motorola to SceneDoc, a Mississauga, Ontario, startup that has created a so-called trusted digital notebook. Its mobile app lets police, fire, and emergency workers record audio and video files while scribbling on a digital notepad and delivering all that information in real time.

"Today, if you're at a crime scene, the police officer in most cases still has a little paper notebook," says Schroeder, whose goatee and hipster glasses belie his legal background. He has spent about half of his twenty-seven years at Motorola in its networks division and most of the other half in its venture capital arm. "I witnessed a really bad accident last year, and that's exactly what I saw," he recalls. "I called 911 and I waited. When the officer came to interview me, he had the little paper flip notebook."

How does Motorola Solutions satisfy the "intelligent edge" hunting ground? By investing in a company such as ShotSpotter of Newark, California, which provides gunfire location detection based on sonar technology—basically, intelligent microphones that triangulate to pinpoint the origin of shots fired. Now adopted by many major and midsized American cities, the network can detect how many shots have been fired and how far apart. That helps cops respond faster to a crime scene, with a better sense of what happened.

## CREATE AN INVESTMENT BOARD THAT GETS INVOLVED IN THE PORTFOLIO AND MOVES FAST

Before Schroeder puts any money on the table, he gets a buy-in from several different folks. First is an executive sponsor, a C-suite-level executive, usually his boss, Paul Steinberg, or Bruce Brda, executive vice president of products and services. "It'll be Bruce if the company we're looking at is a near-term fit with the business, an immediate-adjacency kind of thing," Schroeder explains. "If it's something a bit further out—an example of that would be our drone investment—then Paul Steinberg would be the executive sponsor."

Schroeder also co-opts a "business unit champion"— someone "either in the business proper or in the CTO organization, typically somebody at the director level." This is not a casual commitment. "Every day when you wake up, you're going to think about and worry about what we're going to do with the portfolio company and wonder, 'How do we achieve the strategic thesis on which our investment was made?'" says Schroeder.

There's a third level of insider engagement—with a liaison team. It's made up of someone from the business strategy group, the non-ventures part of Steinberg's team, and, most recently, from the go-to-market unit. "This is our go-to team; they help us vet the deals we put through," says Schroeder. "If it's a deal we think could have some merit, then we'll send it to the liaison team and ask them to review it." And if the team "thinks it's worth taking a harder look, the next step is typically a video call with the prospect." And after that, a simple survey filled out in minutes by the liaison people and, sometimes, the target startup. If that suggests greenlighting the deal, then Schroeder and company consult with a handful of engineers to set up a proof of concept. "It's all meant to vet these deals very quickly," says Schroeder. "That's another discipline that has really been instilled in everybody: we want to be fast."

## ROAM THE OUTER LIMITS OF THE HUNTING GROUNDS

Motorola Solutions sometimes engages in a ready-fire-aim approach to venture funding. "I actually like investing in non-pure-play companies," says CTO Steinberg, whose explanations of things are refreshingly lucid and colloquial for the geek that he is, having spent two decades at Motorola, most of that time in the wireless network equipment business. "We stumbled across the startup Eyefluence not really even thinking about eye tracking," he says. "Once I spent time with Jim Marggraff and Dave Stiehr"—the founders—"and they kind of explained what they were doing, it's like, 'Holy crap, that's the answer: I can use my eyes as a mouse.' And so you start to think, 'Well, now, if I put that together with my head-worn display, now I've solved a problem.'"

Conrado pulls back the lens on Eyefluence to provide more context. "Its focus is on virtual-reality and augmented-reality eye control," he says. "You put on its headgear and you don't have to use your hands or your voice to interact with commands." It's great for VR games, which was the original target of the Milpitas, California, startup. But Motorola Solutions saw something else in the eye-tracking algorithms, which can operate in variable lighting conditions. "Think about police officers, firefighters," says Conrado. "They've got to have their hands free. We saw an opportunity to actually go out and test their capabilities for *our* markets." Motorola Solutions is continuing to get user feedback on the proof of concept, which is still in the planning phases.

Another partnership with a different tech eyewear startup has taken Motorola Solutions even further. Recon Instruments, a startup in Vancouver, British Columbia, developed heads-up displays and smart glasses a year and a half before the introduction of Google Glass—and has made a success of it. Recon aimed squarely at extreme sports, mostly skiing and mountain biking. "It wasn't pointed at our market at all," says Steinberg. "But it was the perfect embodiment of what we wanted to do."

Conrado sketches a hypothetical scenario of a cop pulling over a motorist in a routine traffic stop. With Recon's head-worn device, the video starts playing, but suddenly information on the driver pops up on the eye-level computer display to suggest there's an arrest warrant out on the guy—and you don't want to play audio that would blow your cover. "By investing in them, within two to three months, we had a working prototype," says Steinberg.

## BACK A *LOT* OF DIFFERENT STARTUPS TO INCREASE THE CHANCES OF A BREAKTHROUGH

This is a practice that GE has embraced; you'll see that in detail later in the book, in Chapter 8.

Motorola Solutions has also discovered that you can get some-place faster—maybe even a place you hadn't anticipated—by making multiple bets within the hunting grounds. "There's something to be said for that notion of threads of investing, as opposed to singletons," Steinberg reasons. "Because what winds up happening is you start introducing these companies to each other and you make them better as they tend to cluster." Backing both Recon (smart glasses) and Eyefluence (eye tracking), for example, turns out to be anything but redundant.

Why? Both startups offered different capabilities that, when combined, added up to something more impactful: a Motorola Solutions prototype known as "the connected first responder."

As Steinberg recalls, the idea began to take shape after a conversation with a venerable and well-known weapons manufacturer. "They were talking about putting accelerometers and gyros in their sidearms," Steinberg says, adding that after a gun fires, they can so precisely measure the movement of a part that they could tell, for instance, if the slide was lubricated properly. "I didn't care about any of that. They wanted to make the gun a service; I cared about the fact that the gun was now a sensor that could tell me an awful lot of interesting things."

What sort of things? The idea is that a first-responder system, built around a human instead of a weapon, could be a lot smarter and more connected and therefore more useful to people in emergency situations. "If you think about the wearable experience you and I have today, it usually looks something like a device, Bluetooth link, application on a smartphone. If I have two of them, I have that doubled or tripled," says Steinberg, his blue eyes blazing with excitement. But "there's nothing that really coalesces that and fuses it together."

At least not until the development of something called a "context engine." A piece of software that pulls together a network of different devices, it takes input from a variety of sensors and presents the information in its most useful form—in this case, helping responders act wisely and effectively in an emergency. "Think of an emergency situation where a weapon is deployed, the responder's biometric conditions are elevated, and the location is not at the precinct or a gun range," Steinberg posits. "Those three events taken together indicate an action I want to command from headquarters." But how? Especially since most people who are confronting danger can't process more information, even if it's vital to their survival.

The solution: a software platform called "Responder Alert" that integrates sensors into a Bluetooth Personal Area Network and includes a rules engine to coordinate them. The platform is coupled with a body-worn, eyes-up, hands-free video camera that lets cops "talk" directly to the command center.

Responder Alert uses contextual information to automatically control the Si500, Motorola Solutions' body-worn camera, based on real-time conditions—for example, turning on the camera when officers leave their vehicle or deploy their weapon. All visual and audio information captured by the Si500 camera is stored in the company's cloud-based content management system called CommandCentral Vault. That secure system lets cops review and share digital evidence. And it allows them to delete such sensitive data as license plate numbers and faces of minors from video footage—which otherwise can take hours to redact.

Steinberg sees other potential applications for the Si500 beyond law enforcement. It can help people doing construction work, utility repairs, or oil-field services projects. "So it's not guns and batons, it's wrenches and ohm-meters, but the exact same problem, right? It's a team activity, and the more you can share the team context, the better."

What started as a chat with a well-known weapons manufacturer and a couple of bets on different startups doing body-worn video cams somehow ignited inspiration and innovation.

## INVITE EVERYONE AT THE COMPANY TO PITCH USEFUL PRODUCT IDEAS

At Motorola Solutions, looking for startups isn't just privileged territory for managers and executives, the way English forests stocked with all manner of wild beasts were reserved for Henry VIII's venery pleasure; they're the property of everyone.

To increase involvement, the company has held a number of "Startup Challenge" competitions for employees.

In one competition, roughly one hundred employees suggested ideas they'd like to pursue. These were winnowed to thirty, and of that group, fifteen were pitched to a panel made up of the heads of different Motorola Solutions departments. The winner was a small group that decided to create a body harness radio for petrochemical workers, a hands-free, sophisticated communications device.

Pulled out of their jobs for two weeks, the team huddled with Motorola Solutions designers, software engineers—"whatever they needed to bring it to life," says Sean Taylor, a senior strategy manager who is part of Reese Schroeder's liaison team.

The device is being tested with customers, everything from its utility to its price—all after just six months of development. And what did Motorola Solutions sacrifice for this employee-created enterprise that has a shot at commercial success? A few hundred work hours and a couple hundred thousand bucks. Even if the product flops, there is incalculable value in opening the gate to the innovation ecosystem for the entire company.

## DON'T FOCUS JUST ON THE MONEY

Remember the chief reason that so many legacy companies engage in partnerships? Revenue. The experiences of Motorola Solutions, along with other mature companies, suggest that money alone might be the wrong impetus—at least at the beginning of a relationship. "We don't get too deeply into the financial side of the company because it's really irrelevant until we get a feel for whether this is really strategic," says Schroeder, the venture capital meister. That's one key reason that venture capital is under the wing of CTO Paul Steinberg, rather than

Motorola Solutions' finance group or its product development teams.

Many of these partnerships go on for at least five and up to eight or ten years. By not imposing profit and loss (P&L) expectations too soon, Motorola Solutions has done well. Schroeder reckons that of the 200-plus investments since the corporate fund started, "I think only six or seven resulted in no return of capital to the corporation." That's a far better batting average than you find even among the venture capitalists on Silicon Valley's famed Sand Hill Road. "I want to say we've had at least a dozen IPOs and well over one hundred M&A exits," Schroeder adds.

With such a richly populated ecosphere for new ideas, Motorola Solutions is a little tough to wrap your head around. Put more simply, this is a company built on some very useful imperatives: start with powerful themes that different parts of the organization can act on; look for many partners to back that can help satisfy your goals—and help you land that accidental discovery; get everyone at the company, from the C-suite on down to the proverbial mailroom clerk who might just have a great idea, engaged in your higher purpose.

Whether you tack toward GE beliefs or Wells Fargo's mantra of customer value, Target's Open House, IBM's great challenge, or Motorola Solutions' complex hunting grounds, attach yourself to a cause that's bigger and broader than any immediate gain. Experiment, take risks, iterate. Who knows what sparks can fly?

# 4

## How to Find Your Own Thoroughbred

Serendipitous collisions—that's where magic happens.
—Toby Rush, *founder and CEO of EyeVerify*

Backstage at Orchestra Hall in downtown Minneapolis, a 1970s relic of the Modernist movement, it's almost showtime. Milling about or sitting at one of a half-dozen tables, the performers are wearing T-shirts, jeans, and day dresses, rather than tuxes and gowns. You can hear occasional laughter or quiet conversation, chatter that's part camaraderie, part competition. These aren't musicians or actors, however, but founders of eleven startups who have spent fourteen summer weeks working at Target's headquarters to participate in its first retail accelerator, in partnership with Techstars. Each startup received $20,000 and weeks of intensive mentoring from Target execs and business leaders of all walks around the Twin Cities. Now, on what's called Demo Day, each founder has five minutes onstage to pitch his or her company before an audience of roughly a thousand people—potential investors, executives and mentors from Target, local entrepreneurs, and, of course, family and friends.

Target, in an effort to be nurturing and encouraging of the entrepreneurs' efforts, offered the founders refuge at Target HQ through the end of the year. But most of these startups hope to bag a few million dollars from investors that afternoon, a decent-sized Series A round of funding, to make it on their own, even if they decide to resettle in Minneapolis, which half of them do. So this is without question a breakaway moment for many, freighted with pathos and a little humor.

This ensemble of mostly millennials almost certainly has its characters and caricatures. But it also represents one of Target's most determined efforts to find potential startups to partner with. Linking up with Techstars, which has provided valuable services to thousands of very young companies for a decade, is just one way that older, more established companies can discover startups and test out potential relationships with them. It's by no means the only way to prospect for partners. Once an established company determines it is interested in allying itself with startups, there is still a long process involved in finding them.

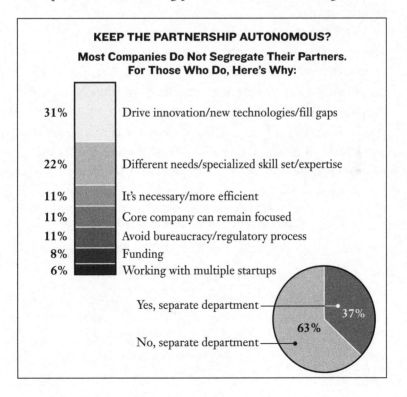

**KEEP THE PARTNERSHIP AUTONOMOUS?**

**Most Companies Do Not Segregate Their Partners.
For Those Who Do, Here's Why:**

| | |
|---|---|
| 31% | Drive innovation/new technologies/fill gaps |
| 22% | Different needs/specialized skill set/expertise |
| 11% | It's necessary/more efficient |
| 11% | Core company can remain focused |
| 11% | Avoid bureaucracy/regulatory process |
| 8% | Funding |
| 6% | Working with multiple startups |

Yes, separate department — 37%

No, separate department — 63%

Most legacy companies aren't adequately prepared to deal with startups. Sixty-three percent of established companies surveyed in the Global Partnership Study said they have no separate department or division for that purpose. Among the 37 percent that do, the chief reason for having such a unit is that it helps drive new ideas and new technologies.

"We're much more focused on innovation than traditional oil and gas companies," commented one vice president from the energy sector who participated in the survey. "We started this department fifteen years ago." The number two reason (22 percent) for creating a detached group focused on partnerships: it requires specialized skills and expertise. "It takes a different set of capabilities to understand the challenges faced along the way," observed a healthcare executive from one of the surveyed companies.

What kinds of things do these groups typically look for in startup partners? A technology match, say 63 percent of enterprise companies canvassed in our study, as that suggests the startup may be an appropriate accomplice to address particular challenges. They're also seeking proven solidity: an established track record (50 percent) and a financially stable partner (41 percent). Four in ten respondents say they're searching for an innovative culture.

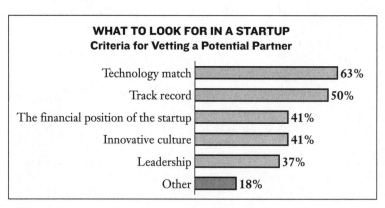

**WHAT TO LOOK FOR IN A STARTUP**
**Criteria for Vetting a Potential Partner**

| | |
|---|---|
| Technology match | 63% |
| Track record | 50% |
| The financial position of the startup | 41% |
| Innovative culture | 41% |
| Leadership | 37% |
| Other | 18% |

The mature companies I've talked with have either a team dedicated to the search, or a group of executives who have taken on that role in addition to everything else they already do. It's part of a new job description for senior executives that would take up an ungainly number of résumé pages.

Still, it's part of the new leadership role I'm seeing across a number of legacy companies. CEOs increasingly realize they need to get out more into the world, and not just to be ambassadors for their companies or to meet with shareholders and customers and employees. They realize they also need to have close encounters of a different kind—with startups and even with rivals, to expose themselves to new ideas, new tactics, different cultures, new ways of doing things.

People often ask me what I would do differently as Procter & Gamble's global marketing officer if I could wind the clock back. That's an easy one: although I was one of the more outward-focused executives at P&G at the time, I wish I'd done even more traveling outside of our P&G offices. Some of my best ideas came from visits with Google (as I discussed in Chapter 1), Facebook, Microsoft, and Nike, trips that inspired me to rethink business, passion, and priorities. Attending the annual Cannes Lions International Festival of Creativity since 2003, and pioneering the CMO Accelerator Programme for senior marketing leaders there, has helped me to recharge and reevaluate my assumptions every year because of the incredibly talented and accomplished people I meet. Yes, it's fun to see old friends and have a drink or two. But what's even more invigorating is to stumble upon a business I've never heard of or an entrepreneur engaged in something inspiring or transformative.

At heart, what I learned is to go out and fish in unfamiliar waters.

So how do experienced legacy companies cast their nets? Sometimes they can reach out via social media outlets such as

LinkedIn. Another way is by attending meet-ups or conferences, including the Consumer Electronics Show (CES) in Las Vegas, the Mobile World Congress in Barcelona, or the week-long South by Southwest (SXSW) conference in Austin, Texas. Still others visit entrepreneurial centers on both U.S. coasts, as well as in major cities in the South, Midwest, and across the world. A few companies rely on people outside the company—often incubators, venture capitalists, and private equity investors—to tap into the flow of startup prospects, or they are approached by startups themselves wanting to work with a more established company.

One common thread among all these companies is that they make a regular habit of getting out of the building and meeting with young entrepreneurs determined to change the work and disrupt an industry. What the best managers and leaders realize is that even a chance encounter can change the life of your company.

## LEAN ON YOUR NETWORKS

John Haugen, who oversees General Mills's incubator 301 INC, meets with lots of food groups. Since 301 INC recently shifted from seeding and building businesses internally to nurturing a small number of startups. "We've been getting a lot of inbound inquiries," he says. But Haugen also leans heavily on relationships he's been building for more than a quarter century for introductions to young startups.

One of the key people Haugen counts on for ideas is Scott Jensen. "Scott is very well networked in the natural foods community," Haugen says of the CEO of Rhythm Superfoods of Austin, whose kale snacks have helped to make that vegetable at least as edible as, well, Brussels sprouts. Haugen also points to CircleUp, a San Francisco crowdfunding platform that focuses

on consumer brands. "They're smart partners, filling the gap in the marketplace for emerging brands," he says. "We've co-invested with them in two of our eight deals." The last time I met with Haugen, he was on his way to the Natural Products Expo East in Baltimore.

Rhythm Superfoods is one of 301 INC's portfolio companies. A onetime ad man, Jensen has been in the food and beverage business since he left Georgia-Pacific, where he promoted Brawny paper towels and Dixie cups and plates. His Stubb's Bar-B-Q—the restaurant, sauces, and marinades—is as much a part of the Austin ecosphere as live music and tech startups.

A big, affable bear of a man, Jensen has been a local entrepreneurial star for twenty-five years, sponsoring events in the emerging food area and offering generous heaps of advice to many young companies, some of which he has backed. He got to know Haugen and 301 INC through Presence Marketing, the largest sales broker in the natural foods category. "I like these guys," says Jensen of 301 INC. "They're out there, they're everywhere—and they're investing in the community."

The lesson seems to be: tap into your resources, whether they're portfolio companies or part of your network, to meet new prospects.

## STEP OUTSIDE AND LOOK AROUND

Wells Fargo is even less methodical, using an open enrollment system for its accelerator program. "Anyone can submit their plans; we get hundreds of them," says Braden More, former co-chief of the accelerator, which accepts half a dozen applicants each year. And despite his efforts to explain what kinds of companies they're looking for, he occasionally gets solicitations from outliers like a wedding planner. "We have a group of folks who come in with a high level of expertise in terms of assessing,

'Does it look like something that could really impact our customers or help us with the business?'"

I asked More who was among the group. He replied, "A network of subject-matter experts inside the company that represents different lines of business. Someone from the wealth management group. Someone in the mortgage group. And we go to them and say, 'We have this company that has this idea, does this interest you guys?'" If it does, somone on that team, typically a manager who makes buying decisions, agrees to mentor the startup for six months, an unusually long commitment, often requiring patience as well as perseverance.

The bank has a long history of trolling relentlessly for prospects. "What are the top ten technology companies that we don't know?" Braden asks, explaining an important premise at Wells. "Doesn't that make you feel a little vulnerable? How are you going to engage with these folks?"

Back in 2012, a member of the bank's tech scouting team was walking the floor of the Global Identity Summit and Biometric Consortium Conference and Technology Expo in Tampa when a sandy-haired thirty-seven-year-old from Kansas contacted him. "I jumped out in front of him," recalls Toby Rush, founder and CEO of EyeVerify, the biometric security startup I discussed in Chapter 3.

Wells Fargo was looking for the kind of technology Rush had developed: a mobile, eye-based verification of identity to replace passcode IDs for bank accounts, something that was reliable, accurate to ridiculous standards, and easy to use. Rush's system was pretty good on the first two. But "our user experience was really bad, wonky," Rush admitted. Wells Fargo, he says, was intrigued by the software and wanted to stay in touch, but gave him "two or three big nuggets to crack."

Solving them ended up taking two years. Roughly a year into revamping the company, Rush thought he and his development team had cracked the problem, until a small pilot program brought them to a halt. There was a problem: In order to take a selfie to capture the deep veins in the whites of your eye, you had to look up and to the left to expose more blood vessels. Users found that weird and awkward. So EyeVerify reached a critical juncture: it either had to figure out how to get a good enough scan of the sclera when someone looks straight into the phone's camera or fold up shop.

Rush's team plugged away on image enhancement and improvements in the algorithms and came up with a more workable model. Rush's technology was embraced by Wells Fargo Labs, and then Rush was invited to be among the first entrants in the accelerator. In June 2016, the bank started rolling out EyeVerify's eyeprint technology to select commercial customers. Three months later, the company was acquired by Alibaba Group, China's e-commerce emporium, for a reported $100 million.

Rush continues to work with Wells Fargo and other financial institutions. His advice to executives at other legacy companies? "Get out a lot. Serendipitous collisions, unexpected collisions—that's oftentimes where the magic happens."

## DON'T POOH-POOH SOCIAL MEDIA

Though it forages widely for its hunting grounds, Motorola Solutions is always looking for new entry points to find fresh ideas and new faces, including such familiar sites as LinkedIn. That's how Israeli startup Agent Vi ("vee-eye," for video intelligence) reached out to Reese Schroeder, Motorola Solutions' venture capital czar.

The Tel Aviv company makes video analytics software for the security and safety industries, Motorola Solutions' sweet spots, by providing real-time surveillance and alerts. They also offer the ability to search automatically for archived video—an indispensable tool for law enforcement as well as business intelligence. "Itsik Kattan, the CEO, sent me a message through LinkedIn," Schroeder recalls. "We then arranged to meet at the ISC West Conference," the International Security Conference and Exposition in Las Vegas.

## PUT ON EVENTS AND INVITE THE MULTITUDES

Watson—IBM's cognitive computing platform—is a magnet for startups hoping to turbocharge their businesses. And because IBM is always on the prowl for new apostles, it holds lots of Watson-related events around the world, offering its artificially intelligent wares to companies. One of those events helped turn Arthur Tisi, cofounder of Connectidy, into a "missionary." People shouldn't be afraid of machine learning and artificial intelligence, he says. "This is not a dystopian, Orwellian thing." Even when it comes to a dating app.

Tisi is in his mid-fifties, and usually sporting a leather jacket, jeans, and tinted glasses, which give him a vaguely Bono-ish air. Perhaps that is not a surprise: Tisi is a musician, as well as a tech aficionado with a list of startups as long as U2's greatest hits. His current gig is a holding company, Praescripto Group, which acts as an umbrella for different ventures into cognitive computing, machine learning, and robotics engineering. But what currently knits him most closely to IBM is Connectidy, his dating app that leverages several of Watson's capabilities, including Personality Insights and Tone Analyzer, tools that exploit linguistic analysis to "read" your feelings, social behaviors, and language style.

In this case, Connectidy is using Tone Analyzer and has created a product they have branded as "Spell Check for Your Emotions" "to identify somebody's needs, values, personality, and purpose for relationships." Says Tisi, "We help people understand their personality, their needs, and their values so that they can make better choices. The more information you provide the app, the better it gets," and the more surprises of self-discovery.

Filtering text via your social media sites, Connectidy analyzes your communication style—which is trickier than one might suppose. "When you communicate with somebody, you think you're conveying something accurately 80 percent of the time, while they're responding 20 percent of the time with that degree of accuracy," says Tisi.

Connectidy constructs a personality profile along the lines of the so-called Big Five model—things like how open, conscientious, extroverted, agreeable, and neurotic you are (also referred to as the OCEAN or five-factor model)—and uses Tone Analyzer to locate you on the spectrum of joy, fear, transparency, and confidence. It's all designed to help you make better, more informed choices about whom to date. The last component is a rating system—think the five stars on Yelp or Uber—where you can leave feedback, or receive it to learn after a first date that, say, you came across as rude or awkward or wonderful. All in all, rather more thoughtful than the snarky drive-by dating app Tinder.

Still, IBM was cagey at first, worried about wading into the realm of personal relationships. Tisi approached one of his advisors, Brenda Dietrich, an IBM Fellow and a vice president in its research divisions, as well as one of its top patent holders. "She was like, 'Arthur, they're never going to go for it, but they should do it,'" he recalls. But Big Blue surprised him. It's a different and more open company since Tisi first got involved with IBM in 2009. And just after Valentine's Day in 2016, Connectidy and IBM announced their company's engagement.

## RISK SOMETHING NEW

Executives at Target do more than their share of seeking out promising startups. Gene Han, whom I introduced in Chapter 3, often flings open the doors at Target's San Francisco Open House to Bay Area entrepreneurs who are curious about what it's like to work with a major national retail chain. By turning Open House into a hangout for founders, Han can keep up with important new trends, ideas, and talent—and expose Target to potential future business.

Naomi Kelman, the CEO of Willow, heard about the meet-ups and reached out to Han and Open House. A former Johnson & Johnson executive, Kelman had recently launched Willow, which was developing a smart, silent, wireless breast pump, launched in spring 2017. "It was the most innovative product I've ever seen," according to Han. Kelman, he says, had no plans to talk to other companies about a partnership during stealth-mode development. But when she heard about Open House's meet-up, she contacted Han via a mutual friend at New Enterprise Associates, the venture capital firm.

Its retail accelerator with Techstars represents new territory for Target. (Techstars, on the other hand, has partnered with dozens of mature companies.) Target announced the program in January 2016, without much idea of what to expect. Roughly five hundred startups from forty-five countries applied. A first review of the candidates tossed out two-thirds. "We did this whole road show, meeting with companies in five cities in a month and a half," recalls Ryan Broshar, a managing director at Techstars, who oversees the accelerator. "We held six different webinars." By then the number of candidates had dropped to around one hundred. From that group, Broshar and Kristin Nielson, director of innovation at Target, and their teams, picked seventy-five candidates to interview over Skype during an intense week. Another winnowing cut the group to thirty-five, and finally down to sixteen. The finalists flew into Minneapolis for a face-to-face meeting with Broshar, Nielson, and several other Target leaders. The final cut came down to eleven startups; the founders of those eleven would spend fourteen weeks in Minneapolis, getting coached by experienced executives ("Mentor Madness"), executing an accelerated growth plan, and meeting weekly benchmarks ("Big Rocks"). The group finally ended up onstage at Orchestra Hall for Demo Day.

I want to focus on two of those young companies over the next few pages because the founders have compelling stories—and because they illustrate the potentially rich catch an enterprise company can harvest by throwing out a wide net.

## EXPLOIT AN ACCIDENTAL DISCOVERY

Starting pitcher on Demo Day was Carlos Moncayo Castillo, one of three brothers from Ecuador who founded a company called Inspectorio, which provides transparency to the global supply chain. Its platform offers real-time information to retailers and brands about the quality of goods produced at hundreds of clothing and textile plants around the world. It offers an up-to-the-minute account of whether those factories are in compliance with environmental and labor-practice standards.

Carlos happened upon the retail accelerator by reading a story in TechCrunch, an online news site that covers technology. So he and his brothers, Luis and Fernando, applied to Techstars, jumped through the requisite hoops, and flew in for the final round of interviews.

Fernando, as managing director overseeing sales and marketing, made the trip from Quito, Ecuador's capital. Luis, chief operating officer, came in from Hangzhou, in China's Zhejiang province. Carlos, the CEO who manages the development team, flew in from Ho Chi Minh City, in Vietnam. Why was this trio—today wearing identical gray polo shirts with the company logo—so scattered geographically?

The story really starts with their father, who was a pilot but who had "always wanted to be an entrepreneur," says Carlos, whose open and handsome face could thaw a banker's heart. "He tried all kinds of different ventures—handicraft shops, selling flowers, raising pigs—and he always made us a part of the business. I remember being six or eight years old and he was asking me for my ideas." The entrepreneurial bug bit the whole family. By the time Carlos was in high school, he and his older brothers were running their first startup, an online networking service for professionals, a crude precursor to LinkedIn that raised around $600,000 in financing before it folded in the dotcom implosion.

Not long after, Carlos went to law school in Ecuador, completing his final year at Willamette University in Salem, Oregon, where he worked as a research assistant for a professor with connections to East China University of Law and Politics. As a result, he landed in Shanghai. While there, he represented Latin American clients who had legal claims against Chinese manufacturers for defective goods. "We started thinking we could provide sourcing services to companies to ensure that things get done properly," Carlos explains. And that idea resulted in the Asiam Business Group, founded in 2004 by the three brothers. Over the next few years, at least one of them spent a lot of time on factory floors, doing pre-shipment inspections of toys, machines, you name it, before deciding to specialize in apparel. Eventually the company expanded beyond China to include factories in India, Vietnam, Pakistan, and Bangladesh. "As the business grew, the complexities increased," says Carlos, whose postgraduate years at Stanford and Northwestern didn't quite eliminate the accent in his English.

That complexity was sparked largely by fast fashion, which drastically compresses the time it takes for trendy clothes to move from the catwalk to store shelves. "Shorter time leads and more minimum ordered quantities—that's not really efficient for large factories, which generally are the most compliant," Carlos explains. As a result, clothing manufacturers tend to outsource to small, nearby workshops, where fewer controls exist. "When you want to intervene in a complex system, you have to look for what they call 'the acupuncture points'—the points you can actually touch that will generate the highest impact on the system. And you have to identify the actors who are actually triggering those interventions." Namely, the quality inspectors, who focus on a single job: whether a shirt or shoe is sufficiently well made.

The limitation of those inspectors was laid out in stark detail during a trip to Dhaka, the capital of Bangladesh and home to many a factory crammed with dirt-cheap labor. Carlos was following up on complaints of long delays and poor quality. "I arrived at the factory and was shocked at what I was seeing. The workers were mistreated; there was pollution emptying into the river next door. People didn't look well; there was a lot of suffering all around." When he asked the three inspectors about it, they said, "'If you want to monitor compliance, then send auditors, compliance verifiers; my mandate is quality.'" And thus Inspectorio was born.

The platform gives inspectors the ability to perform more accurate, secure, and faster work, and extends their mandate to include compliance verification of workplace conditions. Each factory visit adds something vital to the system. "We have an

adaptive process that adjusts based on the findings of the in-
spector," says Carlos. It then compares those findings to his-
torical data. As for accountability? "We can identify the beta
that exists between self-inspection reporting and independent
inspections." Inspectorio can use those gaps to create a credibility index for each factory and, on top of that, develop industry standards. Retailers have the power to act at any moment
because they "have full visibility about what is happening at the
factory at any point of time—not days later, but the second the
data is uploaded."

So was Target's accelerator helpful to Inspectorio? What
the three brothers learned was how to make a much more scal-
able business. "When we first arrived, we were more like a service company offering inspection services," says Luis. "But we
soon realized we could transform the company from a service
provider into a SaaS [software as a service] business," one that
provides a software platform, which has a far bigger potential
customer base. Adds Fernando, "The progress we have been
making here over the last three months," thanks to mentoring
from executives such as Target CEO Brian Cornell, is something that "would probably have taken us three years." Fernando is such a believer that he decided to decamp from Quito
and move the sales and marketing team to Minneapolis. In early
2017, Target helped the trio raise $3.7 million in seed funding.

## TURN A PROBLEM INTO AN OPPORTUNITY

Jacqueline Ros, CEO and cofounder of Revolar, doesn't plan to
move to Minneapolis. But she quickly acknowledges her debt to
the program, which helped her grow "from prototype to nation-
wide retail launch in eight months." Revolar makes a wearable
alert system for women to help ward off sexual assault. The device connects to a smartphone via Bluetooth; its GPS gives out

the user's exact location. You can send an amber alert (two clicks of the device) or a red alert (three clicks) to up to five friends, prearranged contacts who know just what to do—for example, call you or the police. Given the prevalence of sexual attacks on campuses and in cities, Revolar seems to have a ready audience.

Like many startup products, Revolar emerged from personal struggles. "I started Revolar because my little sister was assaulted twice before the age of seventeen," says Ros. "She taught me that a cellphone is not the right form factor for a safety product. You really need that discretion in order for it to succeed." The $99 gadget, roughly the size of a domino, can be worn under a garment or on a keychain.

Ros was already a Techstars graduate (Boulder, Colorado, class of 2015) when she applied to the Target accelerator. But she's still an unlikely find for the retailer—and an even more unlikely entrepreneur. Born in Colombia, Ros grew up in Miami. After college she went into Teach for America, working at a low-income school, AXL Academy in Aurora, Colorado, teaching Spanish to nearly three hundred kids ranging in age from pre-K to fourteen years old. That's where she met her co-founder, Andrea Perdomo, another Colombian-born American. In her next job, Ros did opposition research for a political consulting firm—a chapter you won't find on her résumé. "I've always been a voracious learner," she says of her career hops.

She gives an exceedingly polished presentation onstage that afternoon. She hopes to raise at least $5 million (Revolar has already banked $3.5 million since it launched in March 2013). It doesn't hurt that she has a radiant smile that could illuminate a darkened room.

So what is Target getting from Ros, the Moncayo brothers, and the other accelerator grads? Half have launched pilot programs with the retailer. Besides Revolar and Inspectorio, they include an artificial intelligence system to help retailers forecast trends and inventory (Nexosis of Westerville, Ohio); a voice-powered search-and-discovery app similar to Amazon's Alexa (AddStructure, Chicago and New York); and a scheduling app that lets hourly workers exchange messages and trade shifts (BranchMessenger, Los Angeles).

The mature companies with acceleration programs that we've visited have one thing in common: they're all willing to take chances, to upend their normal routines by getting away from headquarters and by experimenting with different methods of outreach that have unpredictable outcomes. They include chance encounters with a farm boy who could solve a biometrics puzzle (Wells Fargo), an Israeli outfit with breakthrough analytics for video surveillance (Motorola Solutions), and a startup applying cognitive computing to personal relationships (IBM). All have brought new and potentially lucrative opportunities to a legacy organization.

"You could look at the companies we had in our accelerator program and say they drew the golden tickets," Cornell says. "But that's far from the truth. We benefited every bit as much as they did, and probably more." Throughout the experience, Cornell said, the program highlighted many of Target's best attributes—its brand-building prowess, market reach, and immense scale. But it also exposed some of Target's weaknesses. Decision-making often occurred too slowly for startups whose funding window was measured in weeks or months. Organizational silos could leave good ideas stranded between departments, meaning that partners ping-ponged from manager to manager in search of answers and champions.

But most important, the program helped managers refresh their spirit of optimism and entrepreneurialism. "As a culture, we'd become very good at shooting holes through ideas and figuring out the many ways something wasn't going to be 'right for Target,'" Cornell says. "Yet working with these leaders and watching them start the conversation by asking 'what-if' became incredibly energizing and invigorating."

There can be innovation magic in serendipitous collisions—if you're willing to encourage them and see what happens.

# 5

## Setting Up the Partnership

We would like to be seen not just as a tool in your chest, but as a lever for change.

—AARON LEVIE, *cofounder of Box Inc.*

THE CALL CAME FROM THE SENIOR VICE PRESIDENT OF THE Information and Analytics Group at IBM, Bob Picciano. Big Blue wanted to talk. Most startup founders would've been elated, maybe even quaking a little in their designer sneakers.

Not Aaron Levie. "We were quite skeptical because we had done casual conversations with IBM over the prior eight years," says Levie. "Basically every technology company in the industry we're talking to once every year or two about, 'Hey, are there interesting things we could do together?' or whatever." In other words, it sounded like another in a long parade of "Yeah, sure" conversations that started with a bang and ended with an eye roll and a disconnect.

Box Inc. is what's known as an enterprise cloud company. Its platform allows individuals and companies to store, access, manage, and share scads of electronic files and documents in its army of servers. While most of its more than forty-five million registered users pay nothing for the service, large organizations—and there are tens of thousands of them—pay hefty fees based on their number of users and size of cloud storage. That has fueled top-line growth to about $400 million for 2016, along with large investments in infrastructure. As much mightier competitors including Amazon, Google, and Microsoft flex their muscles in the cloud, Box has to keep pouring more and more resources into its business.

Born in 2005 during Levie's junior year at the University of Southern California, Box is a redoubtable competitor whose potential is still evolving. Like many promising upstarts, its aura is somewhat larger than its income statement. As if to underscore its room-to-grow character, it recently moved to a 334,000-square-foot building in downtown Redwood City, California. When I visited its new glass-walled offices, with giant turquoise-and-white billboards and big video screens, it was stretching to fill the four floors.

## WOO YOUR PARTNERS, WIN THEIR TRUST

Levie decided to meet with IBM in late 2014—but with reluctance. "Do we really need to fly to New York just to have this meeting?" he asked his colleagues. "Why don't we just do it as a phone call?" Still, the Box executives got on a plane and, exchanging their comfortable T-shirts for button-downs, sat with a handful of people from one of America's biggest companies. "We had a two- or three-hour conversation about how we both saw the world, where we thought collaboration was going, where data was going, and they shared pieces of what they saw the future looking like," says Levie.

Just into his thirties, Levie still hasn't shaken some adolescent lankiness. Speaking rapidly, using his hands for emphasis, and raking his abundant hair, piled high like on the young Bob Dylan, and already flecked with a little gray at the temples, he said, "We just put this in the standard bucket of 'Okay, that's a conversation we'll have once every two years.' And, you know, we'll expect to hear some long, lengthy reason why, you know, it's not going to work right now and we'll figure it out later."

He never expected IBM to follow up two weeks later. "We got pretty significant endorsement from their senior leadership that said, 'We'd like to do something pretty big here in a little bit of an unusual way.' And that caught us by surprise. And very rapidly, over a couple-month period, we had the most engaged and concerted effort we've ever had from a partnership standpoint." Within a year, IBM became one of Box's largest customers, along with GE, Procter & Gamble, and Walmart.

Billed as a strategic partnership, the June 2015 agreement integrated Box's expertise in mobile storage with IBM's cloud dominance in areas such as analytics, security, and cognitive thinking to help everyone from medical researchers grappling with millions of academic reports and patent filings to ordinary people trying to get a consumer loan via their smartphones. "They bring a set of DNA and experience that we don't have, and vice versa," says Levie. "We move at a different pace, we build software with a different process, and design with a different set of goals in mind. Conversely, they think about mission criticality and the underlying business process of the customer in ways we don't." He expects IBM Watson, the artificial intelligence engine, to make Box a lot smarter.

What's the mission for this partnership? "Our passion is, how do you change the way people work?" says Levie emphatically. "By building software that actually makes it easier to collaborate and share and access information."

Levie's story illustrates what a successful alliance looks like: common goals, mutual learning, an appreciation of vast differences, and a willingness to bridge them. Until IBM, Levie admitted, "we'd never really jointly developed new products with partners. We knew there'd be a lot of friction, issues that we'd have to overcome. But if we created incentives for both sides to work well together, we could tell a really transformational story for customers."

Levie's encounter with IBM also underscores some of the challenges of partnerships, especially when they're first getting made. In this chapter, we're going to hear from startup partners whose stories clarify good practices for setting up a rewarding relationship, as well as zeroing in on what to avoid in the process. Those practices turn out to be every bit as essential as contracts and term sheets—maybe even more so.

The on-the-ground experiences of startups are incredibly instructive, as I learned from dozens of interviews with young companies and from the Global Partnership Study. While both founders and corporate executives who participated in the survey had positive experiences in partnerships (more than 90 percent in both cases), 80 percent of the startups expressed frustration in working with legacy companies. As you'd expect, the lack of speed and flexibility among established corporations ranks high on entrepreneurs' list of complaints. But when you parse startups' negative experiences in our research, you find an almost interlocking series of failed business goals, incompatibility, and poor personal relations.

The Box example highlights the importance of establishing trust early on. That's not always easy to secure, as you can see in Levie's initial cynicism regarding the seriousness of IBM. I think it's fair to say that most startups are inherently suspicious of mature companies' motives. The challenge for an older enterprise is to overcome that wariness. And the trust has to be mutual and sustained. "What doesn't work is where they've got a hand behind their back and we've got a hand behind ours," says Levie. "We don't know what's in their hand and they don't know what's in our hand."

## CREATE AN ALLIANCE WHERE EVERYONE WINS

Another important lesson in creating a partnership is to set goals that ensure success on both sides of the relationship. Remember, that's the second commandment of Sue Siegel, who oversees GE's Venture's portfolio: "The startup must win, too. Without that, you don't have a strategic partnership."

This is not just a matter of enlightened self-interest or alignment of goals. It's an issue of respect as well. Among those startups that reported an adverse experience in our study, most feel dissed by their bigger partners: 33 percent cited incompatibility (the same percentage that complained they didn't achieve their goals) and 22 percent said they were outright mistreated.

## GIVE STARTUPS ROOM TO ROAM

Another theme, closely aligned to the first two—trust and a win-win relationship—is the importance of giving startups a long leash right from the start. That's risky: it requires giving up a measure of control, which isn't easy or instinctive. But if you set out to accomplish good—even great—things, you will have to grant some autonomy as an act of faith and another example of trust. It doesn't mean offering carte blanche; rather, it means allowing space for your partner to grow.

Levie says his greatest wish for his next alliance is that "we would like to be seen not as just a tool in your chest, but actually as a lever for change and transformation in your company, to be helpful in catalyzing how a lot of these bigger companies change. Not just how they share files, not just how they collaborate, but, ultimately, how they run their businesses."

Now that's something to shoot for. Viewed one way, it's pushing the goal of mutual success in a partnership to a new level: treating the startup as a catalyst for change within the legacy company.

As we briefly discussed in Chapter 2, there is quantitative support for aiming this high in a partnership. In the Global Partnership Study, 67 percent of established company executives reported that their partnership with a startup was more likely to achieve success if they were aiming to change the corporate culture in order to make their company more entrepreneurial and more risk-tolerant. That motivation is second only to connecting more closely with customers (70 percent success rate). Aaron Levie's wishful thinking, it turns out, has some foundation in reality.

## EXTENDING A HAND TO BUILD CONFIDENCE

Don White of Satisfi Labs wasn't expecting a phone call, much less a serious offer, from IBM, either. But unlike Box, which had been in existence nearly a decade, Satisfi Labs was basically three guys in a small room. In April 2016, the startup already had a nifty, location-based mobile app that allowed consumers and brands to interact via Q&A sessions—a range of basic features such as where to find things, how to get to certain places, or how to actually connect with a company employee. Satisfi Labs was doing some business with the New York Mets and trying to nail down a deal with Macy's, which kept asking for more details and pressing White and his cofounders on whether their app could scale. Meeting seven dragged into meeting eight.

Then, out of the blue, came the phone call. The guy from IBM "had no idea about the Macy's conversations," says White. "He just said, 'You can extend your product five steps ahead, very fast, with this one piece you already have. Would you like to do that?'" White was stunned. He and cofounder Randall

Newman had both spent time at large companies designing algorithmic trading—White at Bloomberg Tradebook, Newman at Canadian Imperial Bank of Commerce. The other co-founder, Rungson Samroengraja, had run product development at Citibank and Pitney Bowes. "To be treated like a peer by a big, hundred-year-old-plus company was kind of like, 'Well, what's wrong? Why are you calling us? So you guys aren't going to stomp on us?' They're like, 'No, come on in.'" Talk about trust.

## IF THE STARTUP SUCCEEDS, YOU SUCCEED

This turned out to be more than an open-door invitation to tap into IBM Watson as a paying partner. The alliance also helped to clinch the deal with Macy's. Here is Don White again: "So I call the Watson people and go, 'How fast can we sign this paper? I have Macy's on the other line, like, let's do this.'"

Satisfi Labs signed the contract with Watson in early April 2016 and days later completed an agreement with Macy's. Eight weeks later, Satisfi Labs rolled out an in-store personalized shopping assistant, Macy's On Call, at ten stores around the country. Given the challenges the classic chain is facing, this kind of help is well worth having.

Here's how the app works. Once you're in a Macy's store, a prompt encourages you to type in a question along the lines of "Where can I find a red polo shirt?" or "Where are the restrooms on this floor?" Up pops the answer, thanks to Watson's cognitive computing and the Satisfi platform's geolocation messaging software. Starting with the answers to about two thousand questions, the platform is designed, like all artificial intelligence, to learn new information based on customer use. So far, not bad: the help is a little elementary, perhaps, but probably as good as you typically get from a sales associate these days—if you can find one.

White explains that the platform is only in the first of several phases that will reshape the experience of in-store shopping. "Phase two is 'I'm looking for a red shirt.' The follow-up question from Macy's On Call is 'What kinds of shirts do you like?' Or 'Who are you shopping for?'" And the more the system learns, the more advice-related questions you can ask, such as: "I'm going to a party, what should I wear?"

The idea is to create information that's personally relevant. White says he's in discussions with a very large mall, which he declines to name, on a holiday advice case. "I walk into a mall where there's a lot of stores, and I'm looking for a gift for my mom. There have to be some questions that narrow it down. 'Can you name some brands your mom likes? Or some activities your mom likes to do?' By the time you get down to it, we're basically having conversations through a digital experience that narrows to exactly what I want and need. And then, how do I get there?"

In other words, Satisfi Labs is shining a light on the challenge of locating inventory and delivering the goods. White says this is a problem that can't be completely solved by Watson alone; retailers, which generally don't yet have the ability to conduct real-time store inventory, will have to help figure it out on their ends. That said, Macy's On Call is already bringing changes to the chain. "It could not only affect store layouts," says White, "it could affect store buying, inventory."

His partnership with Watson is galvanizing Satisfi Labs. "It forces us to develop faster," White says. "It's like having our own little development team of ten thousand people building stuff for us." Although, he stresses, "a lot of it's do-it-yourself." That's allowed Satisfi Labs to branch out from retail into apps for Broadway theaters, sports teams, aquariums, and grocery chains. An added plus: as an IBM partner, White gets a boost when he calls on other IBM customers. "They go, 'Can we chat? Macy's trusts you and IBM trusts you, so we trust you.' And I was like, 'Hey this is great. How do we do this ten more times?'"

White's success is pushing IBM into new areas of enterprise where it's never gone.

## HELP YOUR PARTNERS—DON'T OWN THEM

White, a man who is well into his late thirties but looks a decade younger, has the buoyant affability of the charismatic CEO that he is. But here's one way to change his demeanor quickly: ask him how closely IBM monitors his app development. "We don't feel like we work for *them*," White says, bristling slightly. "This is important because a lot of people that we had asked about when we started this, they're like, well, 'Do you work for them now?' We're like, 'No, we're *partners*.' We proactively have a dialogue with each other on a when-needed basis. There's no weekly call, no monthly call."

That insistence on autonomy is a matter of pride. There might even be a whiff of the poet Walt Whitman in it: "Afoot and light-hearted, I take to the open road / Healthy, free, the world before me . . ." But independence is also an existential necessity for startups, a requisite condition for getting stuff done that can help both parties in the relationship. I've seen that in so many sit-downs with entrepreneurs who have the freedom to develop something on their own and the blessings (and resources) of their established partners.

This isn't just an anecdotal conclusion. It's confirmed by our partnership study, which finds that corporations that invest a startup leader with key decision-making authority are more successful in their partnerships than those that keep that power for themselves. Putting a startup in charge of the partnership yields a 75 percent success rate, compared with 62 percent when the corporate partner calls the shots. It suggests that giving your startup partners some room to wander isn't just good for public relations; you might be amazed at what they can produce without vise-grip supervision.

## ALWAYS PUT YOUR PARTNER IN THE DRIVER'S SEAT, AND BE WILLING TO TAKE THE CASUALTIES ALONG WITH THE TRIUMPHS

Aaron Levie of Box. Don White of Satisfi Labs. Naomi Kelman of Willow. They're all incredibly smart and creative and, to varying degrees, prickly, peculiar, and not easily tamed. But their corporate partners have had the forbearance and imagination to help them when necessary, work together when it makes sense, and otherwise get out of their way.

All that sounds rather grown-up and broad-minded, doesn't it? But giving your entrepreneurial partner more authority doesn't just make you look progressive or help your joint enterprise succeed, as we've seen from the Global Partnership Study. It turns out that giving a leadership role to the startup makes it far more likely that the partnership will have a major impact on a corporation: companies that set up the relationship with the outside partner in charge are one and a half times more likely to achieve this result than if they put a company executive at the wheel. That's an astonishing conclusion once you let it sink in. And it requires nothing less than an act of faith.

The takeaway? Spend the time courting your most brilliant prospects. Give them resources and freedom from the start. Enable them to become co-creators of potentially earthshaking things.

# 6

## Getting Through the First Phase of the Partnership

*When times are bad, I'm going to be resilient in hanging in there.*

—DEBORAH KILPATRICK, *CEO of Evidation Health*

YOU'VE BOTH SIGNED THE CONTRACTS, AND THE RESPECTIVE legal teams have shrunk back into their corners. Those of you at the legacy company have picked your team that will engage with the startup founders. Now, how do you host the partnership? Do you keep it separate from your organization, perhaps even off campus, to insulate it and keep it far away from the slings and arrows within your corporate culture? Or do you embed it somewhere within your company?

There's no easy answer to those questions. One surprising conclusion from the Global Partnership Study is that a separately branded partnership division within a corporation is 72 percent more likely to have a major positive impact on the company as a whole than one created apart from the organization. Sometimes, though, that enclave-like structure isn't feasible for practical, legal, or other reasons. But that's not necessarily fatal to a partnership's ultimate success.

Creating the right habitat for the partnership, however, is absolutely essential. What do I mean by that?

I wrote in Chapter 5 on the urgency of giving the startup a great deal of freedom—sometimes an uncomfortable amount. I take nothing away from that imperative by suggesting that you also need some structure, a degree of oversight from a dedicated and high-level team that is constantly accessible to the startup and willing to provide resources, expert advice, moral support, and—at all times—open portals of communication in order to take on unexpected challenges. This group needs to be lithe, flexible, and willing to make or weigh in on decisions *quickly*. And, of course, the group and the startup need to be in sync about overall goals.

Research from our global study confirms these conditions. Startups say that the number one barrier to working with older, established companies is bureaucracy and slow decision-making (25 percent), followed by an inability to get to the right people in the organization (13 percent), suggesting a lack of committed ambassadors (who sometimes mysteriously come and go). The

**BARRIERS TO A GOOD PARTNERSHIP**
**Why Companies Get Frustrated by Startups**

| | |
|---|---|
| 17% | Unrealistic/unmatched expectations |
| 11% | Disconnect/lack of communication |
| 11% | Corporate culture differences |
| 9% | Slow pace |
| 9% | Staffing/internal issues |
| 6% | Speed of decision-making process |
| 6% | Learning curve/lack of experience |
| 6% | Governance & rules |
| 6% | Financing/funding |
| 6% | Lack of communication/shared goals/alignment |
| 12% | Other |

leading causes of frustration among legacy companies are un-matched expectations (17 percent)—indicating a failure to align goals properly—and lack of communication (11 percent). On the other hand, startups note that after working together well, their corporate partners start to communicate differently (42 percent) and begin to move faster (39 percent)—the two leading changes in behavior.

Calibrating goals and aspirations is also critically impor-tant. Startups who say they were chiefly motivated by shared vision and compatibility report their partnerships were 100 per-cent successful; 88 percent of established companies that had a positive experience in the partnership attribute that success to a clear alignment of purpose.

Here's what some of the startups we surveyed offer as advice to their more mature counterparts:

- "They must have a seasoned executive team who are used to dealing with startups."
- "They should provide a dedicated team of people to sup-port us. Also, they should treat the startup like a team, not first-year business students or interns."
- "Speed up the legal and compliance processes. Be more flexible, take more risks when working with startups, and don't hide behind fifty pages of a contract."
- "They should be made aware that the lack of under-standing of shorter decision-making processes costs the company."
- "Most importantly, look for senior-level advocates that have strong alignment in their division."

There should be a lining up of purpose. Dedicated support. Constant exchange of ideas and information. Agility and accel-erated action.

Let's examine these lessons first through the optics of start-ups, when things are just getting going.

## A CURE FOR WHAT AILS MEDICINE?

From inside a low-slung office building in downtown San Mateo, California, Deborah Kilpatrick and her team are hatching a revolution in healthcare. By tapping into patient-owned data with patients' consent, "We're able to tell healthcare buyers what works and what is not working in the population," she says. "That matters if you're a pharma company, a health insurance plan, or a digital health company trying to launch a new product. It matters to the buyers of healthcare and the sellers of products. And it's all about the transformation of volume to value at the highest level."

Kilpatrick is a product of Georgia Tech, which awarded her a BS, MS, and PhD in mechanical engineering (with a concentration in bioengineering). Her company, Evidation Health, quantifies the clinical and economic impact of digital health technologies, an incipient but burgeoning business that absorbs $4 billion to $5 billion a year in investments.

And what is digital health? A lot of different (and sometimes interconnected) things. It's electronic medical records that you can access online and can choose to share with other physicians, companies, or research institutions. It's data that your insurance company and employer collect on you through incentive programs—losing weight, quitting smoking, joining a gym, and so on. It's any of the thousands of health- and fitness-related apps out there to help you reach certain goals. It's wearable devices like those from Fitbit, Misfit, Jawbone, and Garmin that connect to your mobile phone. It's smartphone apps like Apple HealthKit, MyFitnessPal, and AutoSleep. It's data from medical devices, lab work, and clinical trials. It's even data from startups that collect DNA, like 23andMe and Ancestry.com. It's tele-monitoring and analytics for clinicians treating various diseases or, say, offering nutrition counseling.

Evidation isn't pushing on one end of this or another. It examines whether digital health technologies are delivering an actual clinical or economic benefit to patients and healthcare providers—and it does so by collecting and analyzing data that comes not just from the hospital or clinic, but from people at home. Utilizing multi-channel data streams in these studies, Evidation Health can help doctors (as well as drug companies, medical device makers, and insurance carriers) start to offer precisely targeted medicine and other therapies.

Kilpatrick walks through some examples. A digital health company with a new mobile app for glucose management for diabetics wants to understand if people are using it correctly (or using it at all) and if it saves money. A biotech or pharmaceutical company might want to know whether patients are taking proper doses of a new rheumatoid arthritis injectable. And an insurance company with a tool to help people manage hypertension may want feedback on whether patients are actually downloading the app and finding it helpful. Evidation Health can provide answers by getting real-time information from patients who have agreed to participate in studies or to offer data on a daily basis.

Making sense of all the big data analytics is the bailiwick of Kilpatrick's cofounder, Christine Lemke, who serves as president and spearheads Evidation's tech operations and product strategy. Launching her career at Microsoft's Xbox, Lemke went on to cofound Sense Networks, which leans on machine learning to analyze scads of location data from mobile phones for predictive analytics in advertising. At Evidation, Lemke is leveraging similar approaches to identify how digital data streams from the real lives of patients are relevant to health outcomes.

While digital health is still in its infancy, is it too much of a stretch to suggest that Evidation's novel approach could have a colossal impact on the more than $3 trillion that Americans spend every year on healthcare? Given all the problems with the U.S. healthcare system—including rising premiums, the ever-diminishing options for consumers, and the large population of the uninsured who have refused to sign up—there is a heightened need for this kind of information. The future of our healthcare system depends on it.

## SET AND CALIBRATE CLEAR, AMBITIOUS GOALS

Evidation Health was created in late 2014 by GE Ventures and Stanford Health Care (the provider system associated with Stanford Medical School) after a conversation between the two CEOs of those organizations, Jeff Immelt and Amir Dan Rubin. "We were envisioned as a company focused on behavioral analytics and the quantification of outcomes in the digital era of medicine," says Kilpatrick.

Aside from having the blessing of the two CEOs, the company came into this world with advantages very few startups have ever known: an immediate merger with Lemke's company, The Activity Exchange (a robust platform that provided real-life data streams as consumers monitor their health-and-fitness apps), and a $6.2 million Series A round of funding led by GE Ventures. Like Athena—the Greek goddess of wisdom who was born fully grown and armored out of the head of her father, Zeus—Evidation Health emerged fully equipped to engage with any competitor on the digital battlefield.

Kilpatrick ticks off the advantages of having GE as both parent and partner. "Given who they are as a corporation and the verticals"—or different industries—"they operate in and the view they have upon the economy globally and domestically, they're able to see so many moving parts of different sectors of the economy and how they might fit together to create new economies," says Kilpatrick. Although she's spent nearly half of her life working in Silicon Valley, Kilpatrick speaks with a light southern accent. "You have to really understand all that's going on in consumer technology, all that's going on in healthcare, and understand how these two things can come together to create a really brand-new type of ecosystem that generally is referred to as digital health." Evidation was formed with the intention of capitalizing on that very convergence of healthcare and tech—with patient rights and patient empowerment in the crosshairs.

Kilpatrick (the healthcare veteran), it turns out, is probably the perfect person to partner with Lemke (the technology veteran) and run Evidation Health. While at CardioDx, a genomic diagnostics company in Redwood City, California, Kilpatrick helped monetize products such as Corus CAD, a quick and highly accurate test for coronary artery disease. She oversaw R&D and new ventures at Guidant, which made cardiovascular medical devices prior to its acquisition by Boston Scientific—stents, defibrillators, pacemakers, and the like. As a cofounder of MedtechWomen, a nonprofit group highlighting leaders in the medical technology industry, she is a familiar sight—slim, short spiky dark hair dappled with gray, sharp blue eyes, and glasses—at their conferences in the Bay Area.

About the only thing left to chance in this partnership was the way in which Kilpatrick landed her job as Evidation Health's CEO. "It's a classic Silicon Valley story, with paths crossing over very different points in time," she says. Kilpatrick had run into two GE Ventures higher-ups—Sue Siegel, whom we've met in earlier chapters, and Rowan Chapman, who at the time was GE Ventures' head of healthcare investing and is now a board member of Evidation Health—when they were both at Mohr

Davidow, the San Mateo venture capital firm. Mohr Davidow led a Series B round of funding for CardioDx, where Kilpatrick worked as chief commercial officer, and so had to present to Siegel and Chapman on a regular basis. Later, the duo left Mohr Davidow to join GE Ventures, which led CardioDx's Series C round.

In the summer of 2014, GE Ventures and Stanford Health Care began the CEO search for Evidation Health. Chapman left a voicemail for Kilpatrick, asking for recommendations. Coincidentally, Kilpatrick had decided to resign from CardioDx, where she'd spent nearly nine years, but she had told no one about it outside of the CEO and board. She called Chapman back, and "ten minutes in, as Rowan is describing this concept and the person she thinks she needs to run this company, I had to stop her. I said, 'I think this is fascinating, but in the spirit of full disclosure I need to tell you that I'm resigning, nobody knows yet beyond the board, and I'm actually not going to give you any of my network names to throw into your search because I think I might want the job.'" She encouraged them to start the recruiting process, and didn't put her hand up until after her resignation became public information. "The moral of the story," Kilpatrick concludes, "is that every interaction is an interview for something later."

There is near-perfect congruence of purpose between Kilpatrick and her partners. She knows exactly what GE can do for Evidation Health: "They have global relationships they can bring to the table that can get any of their portfolio companies introduced to the right decision-makers at other partner companies." And she's aware of Evidation's valuable assets. The startup's alliances with groups such as Ochsner Health System of Louisiana and Brigham and Women's Hospital in Boston "are big relationships for GE Healthcare," says Kilpatrick. Moreover, "we're giving GE a magnifying glass through which they can see innovation happening at a speed that would be very difficult for a large company." And GE certainly knows what it's getting from her in particular. "I'm a good personality fit, a good skill set—and they've seen me in good times and bad. I want the board's confidence. And when times are bad, I'm going to be resilient in hanging in there."

## LET YOUR BOARD OF ADVISORS HELP GUIDE THE PARTNERSHIP IN KEY DECISIONS

Kilpatrick has certainly leaned on the board to help grapple with Evidation Health's most critical pathways. "One of the hardest decisions we've had to make was what investors would lead our Series B round."

It sounds like a nice problem to have. But the choices were tough, striking at the heart of an existential dilemma for the company. Targeting a healthcare investor might take Evidation down one path; going with a tech backer might suggest a very different kind of business model. "We're a hybrid," says Kilpatrick. "We don't have the binary risk associated with healthcare venture-funded companies. At the same time, we don't have the ability to move at the same speed of revenue ramp as, say, Pinterest or Twitter because we're not a consumer technology platform. Because we're a bit of a 'tweener' between two major sectors, which kind of investor is going to be the most helpful to the company? Who's going to have an accurate view of the company's value? Who do you want around the board table?"

GE, she says, helped her think through the decision. "They see the world through a technology lens. They also see the world through a healthcare lens—and through the lens of energy, infrastructure, and transportation. They can see all these moving parts and understand where the economic drivers on a global and domestic level in those sectors will be in five, seven, ten years from now." Board member Skip Fleshman, a partner at Asset Management Ventures in Palo Alto, also had broad experience with tech and healthcare startups and provided invaluable counsel.

Evidation Health closed its Series B round in October 2016, raising $15.5 million. The funding was led by B Capital Group, a new venture firm cofounded by Eduardo Saverin, one of Facebook's founders, and Raj Ganguly, who spent nearly a decade at McKinsey & Co. and Bain Capital. With a fund of over $140 million, B Capital is making investments in health and wellness, e-commerce, financial services, and transportation, providing overlapping and complementary experience to GE's expertise.

That provisionally settled one identity crisis. But most startups, even those with a clear mission, continue to have them. Kilpatrick had to decide where to focus, in what therapeutic area or areas. "Do I have to work only in oncology—or in autoimmune? Do I have to take all chronic diseases or only cardiometabolic ones?" Kilpatrick and team decided Evidation could perform just as well in all areas of disease, telling any group whether a digital product was effective or not. "The way our software works—and the artificial intelligence and machine learning and analytics—is agnostic to whether a patient on our platform has chronic obstructive pulmonary disease or hypertension. We work anywhere that behavior has an impact on the outcome."

The decision helped Kilpatrick appreciate the importance of what she calls "patient-mediated data"—in plainer terms, the feedback and critical information that millions of people who are on Evidation's platform provide for use in outcomes studies with their permission and informed consent. While we tend to think of ourselves as victims of the healthcare system, at the mercy of insurers, government programs, doctors, and hospitals, Kilpatrick argues that "patients are now coming to the table with a say.

They are the owners of a very important asset in the healthcare ecosystem: their electronic health records and health-related information. The patient owns the data—not the hospital, not the physician, not the provider system, not the insurance company. The patients are the vehicle for how that healthcare information gets transferred into a clinical trial or not." In other words, each of us might have a say in the huge and faceless healthcare system.

Evidation's board will certainly have a role well beyond the first phase of this partnership in answering the crucial question of what ultimately happens to the company. Kilpatrick explains: "If our ability to quantify outcomes rapidly at scale, using real-life digital data streams, is valued very quickly in the market, then we're going to have options." But Evidation Health will probably expand in proportion to the value of its data streams as they scale. "If that happens very rapidly, such that you need capital to keep that investment going to drive value, then some investors would say you should become a public company to keep up with that." Advisors will undoubtedly offer guidance on issues of valuation and pricing.

## BE PATIENT—AND BRING YOUR PARTNER ALONG IN SMALL STEPS

For most people, going to a live sports event is a fun afternoon or night out with friends, family, and your home team or favorite player—along with thousands of other fans, heart-pumping noise levels, and plenty of food and drink you may come to regret later on. Alex Hertel gets all that. But he also sees the stadium experience differently from most of us: as a series of disconnected digital devices, from ticket scanners, smartphones, team apps, and iBeacons to scoreboards, Jumbotrons, and cash registers. Hertel's goal is to link them all together in a way that's engaging and entertaining for fans (through puzzles to solve and prizes to win) and lucrative for his corporate partners (thanks to games that lead to more purchases). With his startup, Xperiel, Hertel has created a way to do it that's as cheap as it is elegant—a simple and fast way to code and create interactive games without the expense of hiring a tech development team.

In Hertel's embryonic business, seeing is believing—but not every potential partner is technically savvy enough to be a believer. So he's had to be selective about whom he shows his innovative platform to, relying on high-powered introductions to get in front of the Los Angeles Dodgers, the Sacramento Kings, and the New York Jets, companies with digital expertise, large fan bases, and an eagerness to make live spectacles more engaging. Even then, Hertel has had to do things in a measured way, careful not to get too far ahead of himself in selling pilot launches to these storied teams.

Xperiel's first sponsored pilot launched during three games into the 2016 season of the Jets, a popular NFL franchise (if not very successful that season). Hertel embedded a game within the Jets' mobile app that allows fans to predict touchdowns while the game is live. You get four TD calls and a chance to win prizes such as game tickets if you pick correctly. The kicker: if you run through those picks unsuccessfully, you get one more chance to call a touchdown—by buying a Bud Light from a concession stand (or retrieving one from your refrigerator at home) and scanning the can's Bud Light logo into your phone. That fires a trigger to give you one more call.

If the experiment sounds a little crude, Hertel is the first to agree. This was a kind of blind date between the digital and real worlds with only a hint of a possibly rich relationship between the two. There was minimal promotion of Xperiel's game besides fliers on the seats at MetLife Stadium and some flashing on the Jumbotron: no Budweiser ads or push notifications on fans' phones by the Jets. During the first game, roughly a thousand fans participated.

One day, however, you'll be greeted by name as your ticket is scanned, with your face popping up on a big board. You'll be able to compete against fans in the stadium as you play trivia games, solve puzzles, and collect digital player cards. iBeacons will direct you to restrooms or to the seats of friends across the stadium. Every purchase of food, beverages, and team apparel will give you points toward new games. And that's just a start.

Still, the results were reassuring: one in four of those Jets fans scanned a can of Bud Light, and the average play session for Xperiel's game was nearly two hours. That's every advertiser's dream of audience engagement. "We didn't expect the conversion rates or the play time to be that high," says Hertel. "From inception to execution was very fast, maybe two months where we figured it all out. The coolest part was building the platform without any engineers, which took ten days." The pilot is just a start—something to build on, something to show other prospects.

Hertel is by nature measured but upbeat, not wild-eyed like some entrepreneurs. Maybe it's his Canadian upbringing or his hyperanalytical mind. He founded Xperiel with his brother Philipp in late 2013 to develop new forms of experiential marketing, on the one hand, and to democratize computer coding, on the other. All that was enabled by the 2010 sale of their electronic payments company, Walleto, to Google (which morphed into Google Wallet), where they both worked for three years as inventors.

When the brothers left to form Xperiel, they had a sufficient cushion to develop some of their graduate school work in theoretical computer science, when the Internet of Things and merging the real and digital worlds were largely dreams fermenting in a few very pointy heads. Setting up in downtown Sunnyvale, California, a Silicon Valley nerve center, Hertel culled a small team of brilliant engineers and Connie Tang, a talented designer at Google who had no coding experience—and was therefore the perfect test case for Xperiel's proposition: create a beautiful and thoroughly engaging game app without any knowledge of programming.

In a large wood-paneled room within the company's second-floor office, Hertel and his engineers draw inspiration from photos lining opposite walls. They're his heroes from science, philosophy, mathematics, entrepreneurship, the arts, and humanitarian causes. Oprah and Walt Disney hang cheek by jowl with Filippo Brunelleschi (who designed the spectacular Renaissance cathedral dome in Florence) and Leonardo da Vinci; environmentalist Rachel Carson and polio vaccine pioneer Jonas Salk with Copernicus and Galileo; Florence Nightingale on top of Nelson Mandela, who is above Bill Moyers. It's not just a hall of enlightenment; these figures celebrate a kind of diversity that is at the heart of Xperiel's mission.

The trend in technology, Hertel says, is increasingly to put more power and ability in the hands of ordinary people. He cites how data moved from mainframes (which served mostly corporations and governments) to PCs (owned by those who could afford to shell out a couple thousand bucks), then to the World Wide Web, mobile phones, and the Internet of Things (reaching more and more people). "One area that isn't democratic is jobs in technology—almost exclusively the purview of elites," says Hertel with a faint echo of his native Canada in his open vowels. "Women are largely left behind. We wanna change that." Half of Xperiel's engineers are female. "Same with inner-city minorities. Silicon Valley is paternalistic, white, elite. We can change that with our technology."

## PACE YOURSELF SO THAT THE WORLD (AND YOUR PARTNERS) CAN CATCH UP WITH YOU

Xperiel was supposed to launch with an app for the Los Angeles Dodgers, timed to coincide with the start of the 2016 Major League Baseball season. As April dragged into May and June, that deal snagged on various details. Meantime, Hertel was dealing with the Sacramento Kings to develop a gaming app, Call the Shot, that lets fans make real-time predictions at the arena or at home. Separately, Xperiel is working on a project to write personalized messages on the Jumbotron in the Golden 1 Center, the new, $535 million stadium that is packed with sophisticated technology and visual displays. That pilot, too, was set back a few weeks while the Kings focused more on the new venue and the team than on its new partner.

Hertel is okay with that, convinced he is getting cumulative traction with his idea. "We take the Jets deal as basically a case study that we can show to the next customer: 'Here's what we did and what we can do for you,'" explains Hertel, whose quiet intelligence and open face—round, bearded, bespectacled—invites confidence.

Hertel believes there is lots more work to be done not just with the Jets, Kings, and Dodgers, but also with other teams in their respective leagues. Beyond that, there are "theme parks—like stadiums, they're gamified, have a captive audience, and a lot of technology," Hertel says. "Casinos, music festivals, and cruise ships, too." One day he will tackle retail as well—when stores become more loaded with technology and consumers are ready for new forms of entertainment and engagement while shopping.

By then, perhaps, Hertel's dream of what he calls the "Real World Web" will have a toehold in this world, where everything we encounter in our lives will have an interactive digital component, all of it connected by everyday devices. Utopian, to be sure. But he has his followers and raised $7 million in mid-2016. Hertel's early backers include former Google senior VP Shona Brown and SurveyMonkey sales executive Brad O'Neill (disclosure: I, too, made a small investment in Xperiel), along with a sturdy cast of seed investors like Andy Bechtolsheim, a cofounder of Sun Microsystems and an early Google backer; Ram Shriram, a founding board member of Google; Intuit cofounder Scott Cook; and Garrett Camp, who cofounded StumbleUpon and Uber. There's more coming: a Series A round for Xperiel is closing in 2017.

GETTING THROUGH phase one of a partnership is tougher than you might think. That initial outbreak of enthusiasm between a mature company and startup, that feeling of how great it will be to work together, is going to need some careful monitoring, cheerleading, and calibration. Both sides require assurance and readjustment so that each is getting what it wants and needs from the relationship. An active and engaged board or advisory group can help with rebalancing—as well as with the most vital strategic decisions a startup has to make—and do it quickly. Buy-in from the top ensures that outcome. When things go right at the start of a partnership, you get a healthy, dynamic baby, like Evidation Health and Xperiel, one that can withstand a few tumbles. As Deb Kilpatrick says, "When times are bad, I'm going to be resilient in hanging in there." But when the goals misalign and important events don't come together quickly enough, the partnership can falter, and never take off.

But as we'll see, phase one is by no means the only time that legacy companies and startups may have to nurture the partnership.

# 7

## Learning to Manage the Partnership

They're far more comfortable with failure than we are.

—PAUL DILLINGER, *head of global product innovation at Levi Strauss & Co.*

PARTNERSHIPS ARE DYNAMIC, LIVING ORGANISMS THAT HAVE to be managed at some level, especially when they veer off-course or start to fracture along divergent interests. As one of Lillian Hellman's characters says in *Toys in the Attic*, an autobiographical play about an unhappy family, "People change and forget to tell each other. Too bad—causes so many mistakes."

This chapter is about some of those mistakes and how to prevent them from swamping, even dooming, a partnership. No alliance is perfect. Each is subject to cross-purposes: strategic misalignment, miscommunication, changing expectations, and different levels of incompatibility. The critical task is to keep those centrifugal forces from overwhelming your chances of success. It often requires some kind of rebooting of the partnership—not exactly a do-over but a realignment of purpose or process or both.

You'll see those themes borne out in stories told by folks from mature companies who've been through the partnership wars. And our Global Partnership Study confirms these anecdotal findings. Even among enterprise companies that generally feel positive about their partnerships, 72 percent say they had to change their expectations about the timetable in order to achieve their goals, and 71 percent claim they had to engage in some kind of midcourse correction. Here are some of the things executives who had to make adjustments told us:

- "The company promised more than it delivered, it took longer to deliver the project—cultural clashes got in the way."
- "We perhaps underestimated what was needed beforehand, which you can only really learn from experience."
- "You learn more as time goes on and you have to adjust plans."
- "There were things we didn't know and expertise that we built. We went to market together and made progress."

Without that flexibility and willingness to learn and adapt, you have an even tougher time rerouting a partnership when it's slipping off the rails.

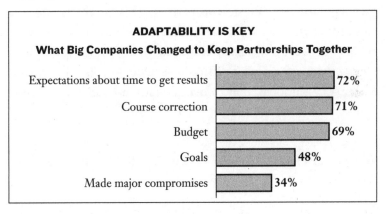

**ADAPTABILITY IS KEY**
**What Big Companies Changed to Keep Partnerships Together**

| | |
|---|---|
| Expectations about time to get results | 72% |
| Course correction | 71% |
| Budget | 69% |
| Goals | 48% |
| Made major compromises | 34% |

## KEEP AN EYE OUT FOR POSSIBLE OVERLAP—AND CONFLICT

Sean Taylor is in his early thirties, tall and lean, with an adolescent's gawkiness belying his decade-plus at Motorola Solutions, currently as product strategy manager. He is an important set of eyes and ears in the startup community for venture-capital chief Reese Schroeder, as well as a business-plan navigator and troubleshooter for portfolio companies—an ideal scout for partnerships that might need some adjustment. And he's keenly aware that today's startup could one day become tomorrow's competitor.

In early 2015, Motorola Solutions invested in SceneDoc, whose mobile app lets police officers and field agents collect photos, videos, audio, and notes while on scene, sending them back in real time to HQ or to the home office, as in the case of an insurance company. Its cloud-based platform is particularly useful for documenting crime scenes and accidents. Based in Toronto, SceneDoc "could be considered a threat at some point," says Taylor.

That prompted Taylor to jump in and nudge the startup to diverge from a strategy that would cross over into Motorola Solutions' plans. "That gets a little bit uncomfortable," he says. You have to tell your startup partner, "You're not necessarily succeeding the way we need you to. But we also have alternative plans because we can't count on you." Both sides eventually worked it out. By late 2016, SceneDoc, in conjunction with Motorola Solutions, went to market with an electronic citation software solution.

## PIVOT BY LETTING A STARTUP TEACH YOU HOW TO DO SOMETHING BETTER

Motorola Solutions has been making two-way radios since before World War II. But it's smart enough to know it doesn't have all the answers when it comes to offering a great product that can sync well with a lot of its other devices. Many of the different gizmos it sells are connected via Bluetooth, the wireless technology invented in 1989 by Ericsson, the Swedish networking and telecom giant. It allows multiple devices such as mobile phones, headsets, and printers to connect over relatively short distances—but not always optimally. Taylor puts the dilemma succinctly, if not elegantly: "Bluetooth pairing sucks. How do we solve that problem?"

The answer arrived from Orion Labs of San Francisco. Orion's chief product, Onyx, is a wearable, push-to-talk device about the size of a campaign button. Press once and you can talk, hands-free, to anyone over Wi-Fi or cellular networks. Onyx pairs with iOS (Apple) or Android (Google-based) devices via Bluetooth, which connects to a network. But it operates on *low-energy* Bluetooth, providing a few advantages: better sound quality, a more robust battery life, and unlimited range. "We'd been working on that problem," says Taylor. "But they're taking some completely different approaches and solving it. If they succeed in that, it's going to help us because we have a large accessory business that revolves around Bluetooth."

So here's a case where Motorola Solutions pressed the restart button not on its partner but on itself. And Orion keeps bounding along, recently adding the ability for Onyx to "talk" to Alexa, Amazon's voice-controlled personal assistant that answers questions, streams music, controls connected features of a smart home, and gives you weather and traffic reports.

Along with Avalon Ventures, Motorola led a $9 million Series A round of funding for Orion in early 2016. The startup's founder, Jesse Robbins, was their kind of guy. Trained as a firefighter, Robbins returned from Hurricane Katrina to help build sturdier technology systems to respond to crises and improve the distribution of humanitarian aid. From there he joined Amazon, where he deliberately staged calamitous events, known as

Game Day projects, to help its websites become more reliable, earning the sobriquet "Master of Disaster."

Robbins went on to found Chef, a software company that helps maintain corporate servers and connect them with massive cloud-based platforms, before launching Orion Labs. Eduardo Conrado, Motorola Solutions' head of strategy and innovation, ran into Robbins while visiting with DFJ, the venture firm once known as Draper Fisher Jurvetson. "Jesse was an entrepreneur-in-residence there and sat in on the meeting," Conrado recalls. "A year later, he pops up with one of the startups we're scanning."

And the rest is history.

In the next part of this chapter we'll explore the details of the Levi's Commuter Jacket with Google's Jacquard technology woven in, an ambitious venture between Levi Strauss & Co. (LS&Co.) and Google to push the boundaries of wearable technology. Jacquard, created by Google, was named for the French weaver and merchant Joseph-Marie Jacquard, whose loom attachments enabled unlimited and automated variations in pattern weaving at the dawn of the Industrial Revolution—a fitting marriage of fabric and cutting-edge technology. How appropriate to these two companies.

Yet the partnership has tested the ingenuity, resilience, and vulnerability of both companies, as what they set out to do had never been done before. And as University of Houston professor Brené Brown said in her wildly viral TED talk, "To create is to make something that never existed before; there is nothing more vulnerable than that."

In this case, you'll learn from two companies that stepped out of their comfort zones, which is essential in any partnership trying to do something original. LS&Co. needed to suspend its assumptions about how it deals with seemingly intractable problems. Google had to respect and learn the complexities of a completely new industry, far from its legacy search business. Let's see how two of the world's most famous trademarks pushed each other to push the boundaries of wearable tech.

## OUT OF A CHANCE ENCOUNTER, BUILD A RELATIONSHIP

In April 2014, James "J.C." Curleigh, an executive vice president at LS&Co. and president of the Levi's brand, went to New York City to accept the Tribeca Disruptive Innovation Award on behalf of Levi's for the 501 jean. Winners that year included the eyewear company Warby Parker, Sesame Street, singer-songwriter Amanda Palmer, and Regina Dugan, who at the time was running the Advanced Technologies and Projects Lab (ATAP) at Google.

Curleigh describes his serendipitous meeting with Dugan. "Literally, I found myself sitting in a small theater in New York next to this cool woman: she's smart, she's strong, she's insightful, and we say, 'Why does it take a meeting here in Tribeca when we live practically next door to each other in the Bay Area?'" The two later found themselves seated next to each other at dinner and promised each other to get their teams together back home.

In my experience, despite best intentions, most leaders don't follow through on these chance encounters. These two did. Months later, Dugan headed to LS&Co. with Ivan Poupyrev, the lead of one of ATAP's newest projects, Jacquard. Poupyrev had started work on Jacquard in January; he and his team built a framework for interactive technology that could be woven into textiles, and they were starting to look for a partner to create smart apparel. Google never set out to create apparel with Jacquard; it sought to build a platform that enabled apparel makers to make something for their consumers. During that meeting, Google shared an overview of its progress and its interest in smart apparel; the Levi's team talked about the brand's shifting competitive landscape and its challenge to become iconic and innovative again through compelling new products. They found common ground in the nascent field of smart apparel.

Curleigh's productive encounter with Dugan would not have happened in the Levi's of recent history. After years of consumer defections, sales on a slight but steadily downward drift, and various missed opportunities to delight denim-wearing women, LS&Co. was finally gaining confidence and restoring its momentum. For the first time in two decades, sales and profits were growing concurrently—and for four years in a row.

Chip Bergh, the president and CEO since 2011, was returning the classic American brand to its roots—"the 501 jean, white T-shirts, the trucker jacket, bringing back cool," as he says—and supercharging the company's terrain with something new: cutting-edge technology. He commissioned the Eureka Innovation Lab, a two-story brick industrial workshop just down from Coit Tower and blocks from LS&Co.'s headquarters in San Francisco's North Beach neighborhood. Staffed with an eclectic mix of people—including artisans, baristas, seamstresses, and designers—the Lab works on green chemistry, novel fabric combinations and production methods, and fashion breakthroughs.

Eureka is a symbol of the new Levi's, "the center point of innovation, evolution, and collaboration," says Curleigh, a tall guy in his early fifties with slightly wild shoulder-length black hair, a trim grayish beard, and expressive eyebrows. He's spent half his life building up consumer brands at places such as KEEN Footwear, Salomon Sports North America, Adidas's TaylorMade Golf division in Europe, and M&M Mars. You can imagine the intensity he has brought to a 164-year-old brand.

LS&Co. CEO Bergh is a U.S. Army veteran who served twenty-eight years at Procter & Gamble, rising from brand manager to group president before coming to LS&Co. You'll meet him again near the end of the book. I know Chip well and count him among my close friends. He's smart enough to know he can't do it all himself. So he put Bart Sights—a guy who grew up in his family's denim factory in Henderson, Kentucky, and whose arteries run blue with indigo—in charge of the Lab.

Jacquard's Poupyrev is an animated, Russian-born computer scientist who helped push augmented-reality user interfaces (3-D graphics and lots of other tricks) for Sony and Walt Disney before coming to Google in January 2014.

Jump forward to the finished product, which went into alpha testing in late 2016 and began shipments in the fall of 2017. Known as the Levi's Commuter Trucker Jacket with Jacquard™ by Google, it's designed at least initially for urban commuters getting to and from work, whether cycling or walking. Its purpose is to let them access the functions of their mobile phone without ever touching it. Part of one sleeve has conductive yarns woven into the denim that essentially mimic the surface of your smart phone: when you swipe that area, your gesture is transmitted wirelessly to your mobile or other device through a smart tag in the sleeve that contains all the necessary electronics. So when you're pedaling through traffic and your boss or spouse calls, you can swipe to connect or decline, tap to change your music, or find out an ETA of exactly when you'll reach your destination.

When I first visited LS&Co. in spring 2016 to begin interviews about Jacquard, the team did not have a prototype available to show me. About a year later, at the 2017 South by Southwest Festival in Austin, Texas, I visited the bungalow where Levi's was demonstrating the technology and showcasing the jackets. The jacket is beautiful, it works, and the bungalow—called the Levi's Outpost—was teeming with people. When I slipped the jacket on and tried the technology, I had that exciting but slightly unsettling feeling we all get when we know things are changing—I felt that with my first iPhone, when I test-drove the Tesla, and sipped my first Starbucks.

The Levi's jacket with Jacquard by Google is indeed an impressive achievement, most noteworthy for what smart apparel—using microcontrollers to interact with gestures and personal data—will change in our lifetime. Not just fun stuff, like ordering a pizza on your way home and meeting the delivery guy at your doorstep, or asking a virtual assistant for directions to an unfamiliar location. But more important functions, like a shirt or blouse that can monitor your vital signs if you're disabled at home and need to communicate with caregivers in a different location or, say, detect signs of a stroke before the symptoms appear.

## TO UNIFY AS A TEAM, UNDERSTAND EACH OTHER'S APPROACHES TO BUSINESS

From draft-table idea to alpha test, the Levi's jacket with Jacquard took a scant two years. Getting there was full of bobs and weaves, not atypical of other partnerships we have explored. From the outset, both sides were eager just to get going, full of excitement and possibility. And why not? It's rare in any career to work on a completely new-to-the-world product. I worked on one in my twenty-five-year P&G career: olestra, the synthetic fat substitute that the company had high hopes for but failed dramatically. But that story is for another book.

Think about it: there must have been something quite fetching about one company in a thirty-thousand-year-old business (yes, archeologists have found spun and dyed fibers from that long ago) making common cause with a relatively new technology enterprise trying to project itself one hundred years into the future. Two companies, both born in the San Francisco Bay

Area, separated by 145 years, coming together to potentially change the role of clothing going forward.

Step inside LS&Co.'s Eureka Innovation Lab and the first thing you see is a neon sign that reads, "THE FUTURE IS LEAVING." It is half amusing and half alarmist. Around the periphery of the ground floor, moving clockwise, you walk past a glass-enclosed conference room with a magnificent table made from gigantic slabs of polished walnut; you see various small labs testing different fabrics, garment finishes, and experiments in digital printing; and a cluster of seamstresses producing prototypes of new jeans over the quiet hum of their machines. Their output is scattered throughout the expansive floor in the center—a large denim crime scene.

Overhead, a four-sided balcony holds samples of what may or may not become next season's fashions. In the middle of it all—advising, criticizing, cheerleading, and sometimes frozen in silent contemplation—is Bart Sights: near-shaved head, tight jeans rolled up at the bottom, worker boots, gray T-shirt, specs that might've been worn by a federal agent in the early 1960s. His hands are stained blue from dye and fabric, etched in darker navy around the nails and cracks of his palms. Sights's compadre is Paul Dillinger, head of global product innovation, tall, tightly wound, and bearded. An ex–Fulbright Scholar in fashion design, Dillinger brings a passionate intellect to whatever he does, his blue eyes seeming to dart with his thoughts. He is almost never without a blue wool cap he wears that gives him an air of both bohemian and French revolutionary. He's been LS&Co.'s point man on the collaboration with Google and Jacquard.

From the outset, Google went in with a specific idea—"a responsive garment, a smart garment," says Poupyrev. His working prototype included novel conductive yarns and techniques that could be woven on industrial looms. The core technology was created by the Jacquard team in Japan, led by designer and artist Shiho Fukuhara. Poupyrev says he talked to lots of companies before landing on LS&Co., eager to see the Jacquard platform integrated into normal, everyday clothes. "They understood they needed to partner with someone who knew the consumer in ways that they didn't," says LS&Co.'s Dillinger. "I think one of the main things we taught them is what it takes to actually make a garment," adds Karyn Hillman, chief product officer for the Levi's brand, a petite blonde whose stints at Gap and Calvin Klein have given her a feel for the business from the cutting-room floor up. "Together, we created the consumer proposition."

Levi's saw the Google platform as a fit for its Commuter line, designed for urban commuters and cyclists. "We could imagine scenarios where a tactile interface could be of value without looking at your phone—what are you doing on your bike? What do you need to know? You like to control media without looking at the screen," Dillinger recalls. "We said, 'This needs to be a jacket.'"

A jacket, yes. But something that doesn't look like a piece of technology, "that looks like a jacket you're going to wear," as Kris Tulin-Roberts, senior director of ideation and design development at LS&Co., puts it. "There was tension in that," says Sights. "I mean, some designers would've let it get more geeky if we had allowed."

One of the early tests of the partnership: the critical factor of timing. Because Google ATAP runs on a two-year timeline, from idea to proof of concept, Poupyrev's team wanted to produce a prototype as quickly as possible. By contrast, LS&Co. operates at a slower and more deliberate pace; that's just part of the process of making a durable, high-quality garment. "We both wanted it to be authentic—nothing gimmicky," says Bergh.

"Together we vastly underestimated the complexities," Sights observes.

"We pushed back on each other throughout the process," says Dillinger. "There were different levels of urgency and different expectations of perfection which we challenged each other on."

## WHEN PROBLEMS ARISE, WELCOME THEM

The Levi's group, says Poupyrev, had its doubts about technical feasibility, so he advised Sights to visit Google's team in Japan and to tour the factory that produced the yarn. He did. Even so, as Levi's started working with those fibers, they failed such stress tests as repeated machine-washing and rounds of scorching, known as singeing. Yarns can't be tested independently; you can only do so after the fabric is woven. LS&Co. and Google did this process together—iterating and improving the yarns so they could withstand plenty of abuse.

"They're far more comfortable with failures than we are," says Dillinger. "The first questions they asked were, 'What was the nature of the flame? Do we know how hot the fuel was?' Google simply saw this as an opportunity to solve another problem. Poupyrev's attitude was, 'Don't worry about the yarn, let's keep going on these other six components.'" Forget about plotting a revised timetable, Google just assumed the problem could be solved.

Poupyrev reflects on the contrastive approaches to challenges and setbacks. "Our main approach to their skepticism was to be transparent: 'I can't answer you all the questions, I can't answer you all the possibilities, all the possible things that can go wrong,'" he recalls telling the Levi's team. "I can show you the team that is creative enough, strong enough, open enough that we can tackle this problem, solve this problem."

Still, the two teams faced a good deal of tension. Poupyrev believes it came down to the two companies' completely different approaches to solving technical hurdles. When Levi's undertakes a project, it works pretty much the same way it's been doing things for 150 years, he says. "They know exactly what they're doing. Like, all the time." Google, by contrast, can be more comfortable with the unknown. "While we have a plan, we don't always know if it's going to take us where we want it to—that's the possibility of discovery," he muses. And that really scared Levi's. It freaked them out.

Yet there was an upside. LS&Co. was learning to think differently about innovation. "People are at their best when they're challenged, rising to new levels," says Dillinger. Adds Bergh, "And it's making us think differently and breaking down these barriers of how we've always done things." Curleigh, Levi's brand president, summarizes his major lesson: "As leaders, we have an obligation to look at the widest landscape possible and find ways to change it. We can learn a lot from progressive leaders like Google. We are a leader in our industry, so if we only look in our industry, we are looking at followers."

This is partly a matter of learning to think and act as outsiders—an important theme in later chapters.

## WORK CLOSELY TOGETHER, BUT REALIZE THAT PROJECTS AND RELATIONSHIPS EVOLVE

Despite the differences in expertise, outlook, and approach, the Google-LS&Co. alliance was from the beginning an amiable, tight-knit group with big aspirations. They shared ideas, work, challenges, meals, and drinks together—like radical students in *Les Misérables*. "There was a small team from their side, a small team from our side," remembers Dillinger. "For all intents and purposes for this project, we agreed to operate as one team.

There was tremendous transparency: no one's hiding trust or petty problems from anyone else; no one's BS-ing about successes that aren't real. Just two groups traveling together, sometimes arguing over expenses for dinner." All the trappings of an ideal partnership: *liberté, égalité, fraternité/sororité*.

Inevitable changes put that brotherhood and sisterhood to the test. While Poupyrev watched over Jacquard, he also became deeply engaged in Soli, an exceedingly ambitious venture to find uses for so-called touchless interactions. Its microchips use radar to detect hand motions that can then control devices like smartphones, watches, laptops, smart-home appliances, and, one day, cars—without physically touching them. Once the project expanded beyond early prototyping, the Jacquard team brought on David Allmon, a product design veteran with experience in production, who joined Jacquard from Mountain View.

In April 2016, Regina Dugan, the head of ATAP, left the company, which led to new leadership in that group and within Google. These changes, along with the expansion of the ATAP and Jacquard teams in preparation for production, were a bit unsettling to LS&Co. Sights and Dillinger recalled how eager they were to hear if Jacquard was still high on Google's agenda. In one of their twice-weekly meetings, the Google team quickly assured them the project indeed remained a top priority. "As a natural evolution of Jacquard, we understand that more partners will sign on," says Dillinger. "But this also left us questioning where we stood in the order of priorities. For example, are other Jacquard customers getting priority delivery of the components that I need to develop the next generation?" The dynamics of the project also shifted with a different cast of characters who worked on it and as more customers entered the scene.

In May 2016 at Google I/O, the search giant's annual developer conference, the commuter jacket was unveiled—exactly one year after Paul Dillinger and Ivan Poupyrev launched Jacquard at the same event. Then in June 2016, Jacquard was nominated for a prestigious Cannes Lions Award at the annual event in southern France for media and advertising, and the team won the highest honor, the Grand Prix Award.

Bart Sights ponders the learning from the partnership. "We can aim for several different successes. Sure, one of them can be selling a lot of jackets, and that's an area where Google and LS&Co. might not have the same target. But the other benchmark lies in solving big problems, such as how to make a washable smart garment."

Whose product is it? In October 2014 Google filed for an exclusive patent of the Jacquard platform and the gesture-control system (it was approved in March 2017). Asked about it, Poupyrev shrugs: "It's complex. We came to Levi's with it—we invented the basic core technology." Still, he says, he considers the project a "co-creation." LS&Co. sees it the same way—even as the technology now becomes available to others.

### LEARN FROM ONE PARTNERSHIP, JUMP-START YOUR NEXT ONE

"How does our relationship with Google affect our appetite to bite off these big projects in the future?" asks Dillinger, posing the big hairy question for LS&Co.—and one that, undoubtedly, a lot of mature companies put to themselves. "Once you get a taste for this, there is no turning back. It taught us to dream a bit bigger. And I know it sounds cliché, but it taught us that all things are possible."

Bart Sights slowly shakes his head. "We learned a lot from ATAP," he says, referring to Google's tech and product group. "We learned a lot from Ivan. And we're already using that in how to make decisions going forward. We've definitely looked at just taking an idea and throwing experimental processes at it."

There's no better illustration of that kind of effort than

LS&Co.'s burgeoning partnership with Evrnu, a Seattle startup. Just as the Levi's brand and Google were announcing the Levi's Commuter Trucker Jacket with Jacquard by Google in May 2016, LS&Co. quietly lifted the wraps on the first pair of jeans made from regenerated cotton (actually from five old T-shirts plus a small amount of virgin cotton), a joint effort with Evrnu. Its technology strips dyes and separates fibers like polyester or rayon from cotton, then dissolves what's left of the cotton pulp and reconstitutes it into new fiber. Dillinger says this process results in a roughly 80 percent reduction in the energy it takes to produce the pants and uses 1 percent of the normal amount of water. "In a matter of ninety days with $60,000 worth of investment, we have the first garment that's ever been made with this type of regenerated cotton."

Dillinger discovered Evrnu at a sustainable fashion and textile conference in New York City's Fashion Institute of Technology. "I said if there's anyone out there who can unlock the chemical reconstitution of cotton—that's the holy grail—please come see me," recalls Dillinger. "And the quickest response was from a tiny startup in Seattle; all they had was an idea." Evrnu cofounders Stacy Flynn and Christopher Stanev are textile mavens with MBAs whose collective thirty years in the business have taken one or the other to Rethink Fabrics, Eddie Bauer, DuPont, Maharam, Nike, Gloria Jeans, and Jones Apparel Group. Mastering the chemistry for separating and remaking fibers, they believe, can be a real business and a boost to the environment. They like to point out that one new T-shirt requires seven hundred gallons of water to produce and that of the thirteen million tons of fabric waste from discarded clothes around the world every year, eleven million end up in landfills.

Those twin goals of doing good and doing well harmonize with Chip Bergh's crusade at LS&Co. The company's focus on sustainability, which includes reducing the amount of water it uses to make its products, is right up there with his goal to double revenue. "Right now, if you walk into our stores, we have clothing recycling bins and give consumers a coupon for a purchase on their next pair of jeans when they drop off gently worn jeans and other apparel," says Bergh. But by teaming up with a partner like Evrnu, "we could take those jeans, recycle them, and close the loop completely."

With that kind of support from the CEO, you'd expect a full-throttle go-ahead on the partnership. In fact, it was a cautious startup. Why? Not for want of enthusiasm from the top. The partnership's deliberate pace centered on the challenges many legacy companies face when trying to scale the lessons of successful partnerships—like the Jacquard by Google experience—across the organization: internal resistance to change. We'll come back to that complication in Chapter 9.

# 8

## Dealing with Failure

Sometimes you win, sometimes you learn.

—AARIF AZIZ, *HR leader for India, ASEAN, and Africa at GE Healthcare*

S OME PARTNERSHIPS JUST CAN'T BE SALVAGED, DESPITE HE-roic measures to revive them.

The causes are as varied as they are in any breakup, in business, or in a personal relationship. In our survey of partnership veterans, we queried the 9 percent of startups that claimed they had a negative experience and found the following explanations: didn't achieve goals (33 percent); incompatibility (33 percent); felt mistreated (22 percent); felt the partnership lacked flexibility (22 percent). Curiously, their failure to carry out objectives is in line with a feeling among startups of being dissed by their uncompromising older partners. What do the 7 percent of legacy companies that had unhappy relationships say about their breakup? While they're less touchy about perceived insults, they complain about exactly the same things: unmet expectations and a clash of cultures.

That finding is largely confirmed by GE Ventures and healthymagination chief Sue Siegel, who oversees their portfolio investments. Asked to describe a partnership that fell apart, she reverts to generic description. "There's a mismatch of expectations," she offers crisply. "It's clear from the beginning that the business"—meaning the startup—"wanted one thing and corporate wanted another. The relationship dissolved in a month."

This raises an interesting point about the *f*-word. No one—and I mean *no one*—likes to utter the word *failure*, except as an abstract concept. The executives and entrepreneurs I've talked to for this book are for the most part humble, courageous, and candid. But, like many people, they get defensive about failure. Despite all the talk (and real walk) about embracing risk, the idea of defeat is still something most company executives have trouble copping to, as if it were an admission of a personal lapse or a humiliating inadequacy.

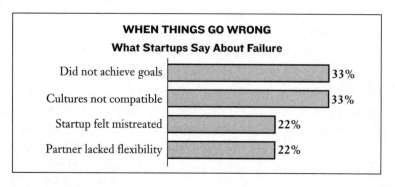

## AIM HIGH—WHO KNOWS?

Will Papa has a BS in chemical engineering from Georgia Tech, but the equivalent of a PhD in failure from the workaday world. Over the last three-plus decades, he's been on the front lines of experimentation and product development, first at Procter & Gamble, where I originally met him, and more recently at The Hershey Co., where he is senior vice president and chief R&D officer. Besides helping to diversify the storied chocolate company into artisanal confections and healthy snacks, he is also persuading others at Hershey to take more chances, bet on the unknown, and seize new opportunities. "Risk-taking is the thing we've called out; that's the biggest challenge," says this smart and jovial executive. "It's easier for R&D guys: nearly 90 percent of transformational innovation doesn't work out—and if it does, we're not pushing hard enough."

Papa spends half his time traveling to meet with new people all over the country. He reads widely among food blogs and food chemistry news, and attends many trade shows. His handful of "innovation scouts" scours the corners of the continent in search of potential partners. Some of those relationships work out very well. For example, barkTHINS—dark-chocolate-coated almonds, pretzels, pumpkin seeds, and the like—and KRAVE Jerky (high in protein, low in fat) were successful startups that Hershey has acquired.

Then there are partnerships with companies like 3D Systems. Hardly a startup, the company was founded in 1986 by Chuck Hull, its chief technology officer, as a pioneer in stereo-lithography, a method of 3-D prototyping built from layer upon very thin layer of liquid photopolymers. Hershey decided to partner with 3D Systems to print chocolate bars—a disruptive process if ever there was one.

Three years of experimenting with multiple new approaches still hasn't taken the partnership to the finish line. "The great thing about the 3-D printing business is you can print anything," Papa says. "But you still can't defy the laws of physics and chemistry. Chocolate is non-Newtonian." By that he means it behaves quite differently under pressure and stress than, say, plastic or metal. "We've made huge progress. It used to take us hours to print things; now it's down to minutes. But to be viable, we'd have to get it down to seconds—and I'm not sure that we have the stomach or patience for that."

There have been other challenges along the way, too, foremost among them a misalignment of goals. As Papa puts it, "They sell equipment; we sell consumables. How do you get the business model worked out?" 3D Systems, he says, wanted both to sell the printers to Hershey and to charge licensing fees. That wasn't going to happen. They eventually resolved that issue, but the technological hurdles seem overwhelming. "With all the brilliant things about 3-D printing—no inventory, made-to-order, ultimate customization—you still can't do it at an affordable cost and quality," says Papa. "It hasn't yet surpassed what you can do with molds." With no regrets for trying, he seems fine if they decide to pack in the partnership.

We're going to spend most of this chapter with GE. Few companies have wrestled with failure so straightforwardly. The industrial giant has discovered that the collapse of a partnership—even a promising one—needn't be catastrophic. That's especially true if you make not one but multiple bets, as venture capitalists do, with the expectation that a few will pay off big-time and that many more will fizzle. The other way to survive failure is to transmute it into lessons that everyone in the corporate tribe can share and absorb. GE does both of these things. Playing multiple stakes and learning from mistakes—these are the themes of this chapter. I'll begin with a failure that unfolded slowly and painfully, and contrast that with a tale of a quick collapse.

## BE CAREFUL WHAT YOU TRY TO SCALE

In the introduction, I briefly touched on this partnership, which went from high hopes to low blows. Now I'd like to anatomize it a bit more before placing it in the broader context of GE's partnership-portfolio strategy.

Founded in 2009, Quirky presented a novel way of creating new consumer products by crowdsourcing ideas to develop and bring to market. At one point the startup had a community of more than a million inventors and was fielding upward of four thousand new ideas a week, according to Ben Kaufman, its founder, whose approach to every challenge seemed to be a refreshing blithe insouciance. By then Quirky had raised—and was quickly burning through—$175 million of "smart" venture money from the likes of Andreessen Horowitz and Kleiner Perkins.

GE had led a $79 million Series D round and formed a partnership with Quirky, giving Kaufman the keys to its kingdom of thousands of patents and new technologies. The idea was to help GE develop new consumer products—under the brand Wink: Instantly Connected—and get them to market faster in big-box retailers such as Home Depot or on Amazon.com. Five months after announcing their partnership, Quirky had produced seven new devices for the connected home, all controlled by a Wink mobile app. They included smart devices such as a heating-and-air-conditioning thermostat (Norm), a switch for lightbulbs (Tapt), a remote control for garage doors (Ascend), a window and door sensor (Tripper), and a personal dashboard to monitor emails, stocks, bank balances, birthdays, time, and weather (Nimbus). Very smart.

Until it wasn't. Within months of getting them on retail shelves, GE and Quirky were hit by a cascade of consumer complaints about devices that no longer worked after Wink was hacked. Buyers reserved special wrath for the $280 Aros air conditioner, which sometimes didn't start up. By September 2015, Quirky was out of money and couldn't support its warranty claims. GE, feeling wary and burned, had long since withdrawn access to its appliance patents. Three months later, Quirky filed for Chapter 11 bankruptcy, and liquidated its assets soon after. GE filed suit, claiming damage to its reputation, but received nothing beyond a lesson in temporarily curbed enthusiasm. It is continuing to pursue its own version of smart-home products.

Beth Comstock, GE's vice chair and head of its business

innovations, puts that experience in perspective. "There are certain learnings, certain cultural learnings, that are maybe almost as important as financial considerations," she says. "In some cases maybe more important than financial." For example? Partnering with a Louisville, Kentucky, startup called Local Motors, an open-source hardware developer, GE has created FirstBuild, a custom-learning center and mini-factory that uses engineers from the local community, students, and GE staff to do limited- and small-run appliances. "We're testing them before we scale them big," she says. "All that started with Quirky."

## TEST IT WITH CUSTOMERS; IF IT DOESN'T CUT IT, QUICKLY MOVE ON

Another valuable lesson from the Quirky experience is the impact of fast customer evaluation of a new idea. The first step is always to talk about an experimental proposition with potential buyers, and if they love it, get it into development fast. If not, cut bait and move on to the next thing.

This "stumble story" comes from Viv Goldstein, global director of innovation acceleration at GE, whom you met in Chapter 2. Members of GE Hitachi—a joint venture partly owned by GE that provides nuclear power plant technology, fuel, and services—were sitting down for their monthly Growth Board meeting to accomplish the not-so-simple task of allocating resources for new ideas and projects.

In this case, the group was grappling with a common challenge for nuclear power plants, which, for obvious reasons, are among the most heavily regulated, and therefore most expensive, operations in America. In this process, the heat from nuclear fission converts water to steam that powers a turbine and produces electricity. The government's regulations for ensuring safety have grown over the years and were not always developed with a consideration of the cost versus benefit of the added regulations. When competing in a deregulated electricity market, this places extraordinary pressure on the utility to operate the nuclear plant efficiently. What to do?

GE Hitachi knew that its approaches—which take into account safety requirements, plant operating data, and the risks outlined in engineering insights—might offer a cost-effective way to comply with regulations and, in so doing, help utilities save on operations costs. Why not offer these new approaches as helpful services to GE customers?

GE Hitachi began discussing risk-informed approaches with clients at various levels and departments. Soliciting feedback from the customers revealed an interesting finding: the proposals drew very different responses that depended on where the customer sat within the organization, with some clearly more receptive to the approach than others. Decision-makers were keenly aware of those divisions within their own companies and, for that reason, were reluctant to engage GE Hitachi in a co-development arrangement.

So, within several weeks of first floating the approach with customers, GE Hitachi pulled the plug. It saved an immediate $500,000 in new-product introduction costs, which, pre-FastWorks, might have been spent without the Growth Board oversight; the risk-informed approach might have continued until customer rejections piled up, amounting to a fairly costly dubious adventure.

Instead, GE Hitachi learned a new way of doing business. Its early testing of customers figured into its ultimate decision about whether to go ahead with the idea. And the full stop early on in the process allowed the Growth Board to reallocate resources to projects with greater customer value—including the twelve other projects and ideas that made it through to the next round of funding.

This was a significant departure from the way GE has always done things. Was the aborted exercise a success? "If your metric is 'Did I build something on time and on budget?,' then no," says Goldstein. "But if you turn the equation on its head and say, 'I'm not creating value and so I need to stop,' then they were incredibly successful."

## AMP YOUR SUCCESSES BY PRODUCING MORE FAILURES

Eric Ries is the lean-startup evangelist who captured Jeff Immelt's heart, helped shape the FastWorks program, and became a key contributor to GE's revitalization. Everyone's heard of him, thanks to his book *The Lean Startup*, his blog, his speaking engagements, his proposed new stock exchange for tech companies, and his annual Lean Startup conference.

You may have heard less about David Kidder, another vital player in GE's comeback strategy. While hardly a shrinking violet, Kidder has deliberately kept his contributions under wraps in order to build enough test cases and experiences with companies to spring himself upon the world and, well, conquer it. Kidder, too, is an author (*The Startup Playbook* and *The Intellectual Devotional*, with Noah D. Oppenheim, president of NBC News), as well as an entrepreneur, angel investor, and early apostle of the digital age.

His current passion is Bionic, a startup he cofounded four years ago with his business partner Anne Berkowitch and GE's Beth Comstock. Part consultancy, part digital platform, the company aims to change the paradigm of how big, complex corporations find new sources of growth. The approach grew out of *The Startup Playbook*, in which Kidder asked dozens of successful founders two questions: How do you select the right idea that becomes a billion-dollar outcome? What did you do in the first five years in order to survive?

Out of their answers Kidder created what he calls Growth OS (as in "operating system"), a novel method of management and decision-making that encourages CEOs to invest in new things the way venture capitalists would. That is, put a large volume of small investments into new solutions to customer problems, knowing that most of them will stumble but those that survive may become pathways to your engines of growth.

At its core, the Growth OS is about a new form of growth management, increasing the odds you are right and on time, by reducing the cost of failure—the biggest hurdle to corporate success. "You have to lower the cost of failure and create a permission in the conversation where the default state is forgiveness," says Kidder, who could be a stand-in for Michael Weatherly, who plays the eponymous star of the CBS courtroom drama *Bull*, right down to the Clark Kent glasses.

Without that permission, Kidder believes, corporations are deluding themselves. "I challenge CEOs. I say, 'Your company leaders don't tell you the truth. They're actually intellectually dishonest—not because they're bad people, but you set up an environment, which you personally own, where they lie to you. Because failure is too expensive,'" he explains. "The only way to actually solve this is you need to work fundamentally differently."

Kidder reasons that the biggest challenges that lie ahead are also the greatest opportunities to help find solutions—and that these solutions have the highest potential returns. "The point is to use a portfolio thesis to meet the future. We're going to take the biggest problems in the world and we're going to deploy capital into bets. Not, like, two, three $50 million Hail Marys a year; we're going to put a hundred smaller bets in the next three years, four years, in that category with a 90 percent failure rate because the cost basis is so low." Bionic turns traditional planning on its head, away from an execution activity and into a process for discovery.

## STRIP-MINE YOUR FAILURES AND EXTRACT USEFUL LESSONS

What does a company get out of so many small failures? The confidence and speed that come from productive learning—the raw material out of which some of the best ideas emerge. "As you're failing, you're discovering, 'Wait, actually that's not the problem—*this* is the problem.' Launch another company; that one's going to die in six months to a year. That's how failing happens. So you don't have to sit back and think of a hundred ideas. The Growth OS is a machine that leads to radically different solutions and business models," Kidder exclaims. "We save so much money by stopping the zombies [businesses that have been prematurely scaled and are failures masquerading as success] at baby level and getting the right things growing," backed by larger resources—people as well as capital.

Kidder has worked with the executive leadership at GE, Citigroup, Nike, AB InBev, P&G, and others in installing the Growth OS. In each case Bionic has compiled years' worth of data on resource decisions the companies have made, from minuscule steps to moon shots. That information gives CEOs an accessible dashboard and playbook of their growth portfolios, letting them see what generally hasn't worked in the past and the decisions that produced those results. But refocusing on a new way to invest—a portfolio approach—engages what he and Ries call "experiment-based learning," where productive failure provides the signals and clues for new growth.

The Growth OS draws on the outlook, skills, and operating mechanics leveraged by entrepreneurs as well as by venture capitalists. Founders have told Kidder that 80 percent of their outcomes are the result of timing and good fortune—a fact of entrepreneurial and venture-investing life. But try telling that to CEOs. They don't want to hear it. "We push the CEO, 'You should be doing new things, now,'" says Kidder. That is, they're pushed to behave more like entrepreneurs, who regularly fail, learn, experiment, and rebuild—and thereby increase their chances to succeed.

What has Kidder himself learned about failure? He tells the story of his own not-so-happy partnership involving his former company, Clickable, and a large strategic partner turned Series C investor. Clickable was a digital platform that let you manage digital marketing campaigns across social networks and search engines, taking the complexity out of optimizing the online advertising spend. Three years after it was launched in 2007, the startup teamed up with a large multinational financial services company to launch online marketing services to their customers, a program intended to simplify the process of placing ads with Google, Yahoo, Microsoft, and Facebook. The partnership started so auspiciously that the company led a $12 million Series C round, giving Clickable a valuation well over $100 million.

That optimism and enthusiasm didn't last, however, as the partners discovered friction on several fronts. "They work at a pace and process that is so glacial that as my company was scaling, we almost fell out of the sky," Kidder recalls. "I jokingly say it's like being loved by Lenny in *Of Mice and Men*," the super-strong but hapless and simple-minded ranch hand in John Steinbeck's 1937 novel whose affectionate embraces—of small animals, the boss's daughter-in-law—always result in a broken neck.

The lesson? "The key to this is you have to fund both sides of the trade," says Kidder, who feels that it is critical to match the commercialization speed of the startup and the partner. He also thinks it's important to accept "good enough" outcomes—aiming for perfection can kill.

Here's something else Kidder learned: if you've got what you think is a big-ticket idea, keep it closer than your enemies. He and his cofounder, Anne Berkowitch—a veteran startup CEO herself, having sold her last startup, Selectminds, to Oracle—are the sole investors in Bionic. Kidder is expanding like a madman, hiring other entrepreneurs and startup veterans while pushing out into an entire floor of a building just a block from Columbus Circle, where the once-mighty Time Warner held sway—until it didn't.

## DON'T HIDE YOUR FAILURES—SHARE AND CELEBRATE THEM

If David Kidder's crusade is to reduce the cost of failures, Aarif Aziz's mission is to increase their value.

The head of Human Resources–India, ASEAN, and Africa for GE Healthcare, Aziz has been with the company for most of his postgraduate years. Moving through its consumer and industrial, energy, appliance, and healthcare divisions, his career has mirrored GE's spread into emerging markets in South Asia and Africa.

Among the most important missions in his current assignment is overseeing the development of primary healthcare centers throughout that vast part of the globe. That means providing not just GE equipment but financing and training for technicians as well. It's part of GE's bigger push to serve the 5.8 billion people who don't have access to affordable healthcare with cheaper, disruptive technologies. (The incubator for preemies described in Chapter 2 is one example.)

"From being a traditional company, which would sell products and service them, we had to completely change and look at a solution that was clearly complicated in terms of its design, implementation, and required skill set, which we didn't have at all," Aziz told me during a long phone chat from Bangalore, India. One example: pairing a state-of-the-art GE electrocardiogram machine with a primitive local device used to print bus tickets. "We realized we needed to have a culture which encourages experimentation much more than the rest of GE." FastWorks, he says, is great. "So why not go a little more and take ten steps ahead in this direction?"

Aziz put out the word to his employees, roughly four thousand people, asking what kinds of things they would propose to promote a climate of imaginative experimentation. "One resounding message we got was about how do you create an environment where it becomes okay for people to share failures as learnings?" The process of disseminating those lessons throughout GE, he says, can benefit the organization and help the individual move forward, instead of "just sulking." Aziz turned to crowdsourcing again and this time asked whether some formal recognition would be appropriate, and got an emphatic yes.

The result is the DARE Award, given to teams that showed enough moxie to try something new and failed, but extracted something valuable from the experience. "The theme we adopted is 'Sometimes you win, sometimes you learn.'" In 2016, Aziz started giving out awards every quarter, with certificates and cash prizes, to small groups nominated by peers across seventy different countries.

## ENCOURAGE YOUR CUSTOMERS TO TELL YOU HOW YOU'VE FAILED

So, who won a DARE Award and why? One went to a team in Nairobi that worked closely with Kenya's Ministry of Health in upgrading nearly one hundred radiology departments in hospitals across the country. GE supplied the X-ray equipment and any necessary infrastructure. "We were very excited," Aziz recalls. "We thought we'd done a fabulous job."

Apparently not. While the installation had gone well and the equipment was functioning, the hospital was still a mess. The chairman of the Managed Equipment Services Committee took the GE team on a walking tour. He pointed out the peeling paint around the radiology department. Washbasins and mirrors that should have been in changing rooms were not there—and neither were curtains closing off those rooms in order to give patients a modicum of privacy. Thinking about the patient's experience "was something we felt we completely missed," Aziz concedes. "But it was an outlook for us to think about, providing a solution completely differently and really addressing the need from the patient side. We learned from that."

## FAIL EARLY—BEFORE YOU REALLY HAVE A CHANCE TO BLOW IT

Aziz's second example comes from one of GE's Southeast Asian teams working on winning a deal for patient monitoring equipment. It was a large order and it required working closely with clinicians in a new hospital that would take the devices. "They had terrific relationships," says Aziz. "They made sure the doctors understood the value propositions of our products." The team waited for the orders to come in.

They didn't. "We lost the deal," Aziz recalls. Why? "What we missed was building and enhancing our relations with the *administrative* team—the people who would sign on the final order."

That was a blow. But it turned out to be a *felix culpa*, as Catholics might say, a "happy fault." It just so happened that another GE Healthcare team in a different region under Aziz had done a great job trying to sell equipment to a hospital's administrative board but had neglected to court the doctors who would use the machines. They, too, lost the deal. But putting together those two experiences, complementary halves of what should have been a whole approach, served as a powerful lesson to GE. "You need to make sure that you're working with all key stakeholders," Aziz neatly summarizes. These stories are being told across the organization.

GE isn't the only company rewarding productive failure. Amazon's founder and CEO Jeff Bezos started the Just Do It Award back in the mid-2000s. Any Amazonians who tried to fix a customer-related problem on their own, did it without asking permission from their managers, and offered a reasonable explanation for the effort after the fact—whether it ended in success or failure—got an old Nike sneaker as a badge of honor, something employees loved to hang at their workspace.

Rick Dalzell, who was Amazon's chief information officer during its earliest decade (Dalzell now serves on the board of Intuit and Twilio), recalls one particular awardee. He was a young guy, just out of an Ivy League school and very smart, who worked in the payments group. He decided to reward some of the company's most active and loyal customers by offering them books at a discount. It just so happened that a couple of reporters ordered the same title and somehow learned they paid different prices.

That turned into a story—and a quandary for Amazon. "I called the guy, had him come up and talk to me, Jeff, and our CFO, and asked, 'What were you thinking?' He walked us through all the things he'd done"—his own initiative, without permission, and a reasonable, well-thought-out idea—"and Jeff said, 'That's awesome, but we just can't do it. Appreciate the fact that you did it, but I need you to back it out.'" Dalzell says the guy went on to do great things. "One failure did not break his neck. In fact, it really started his successful career at Amazon."

## TRY TO FLIP THE SWITCH ON FAILURE

"Experience . . . was merely the name men gave to their mistakes." So said the brilliant cynic and author Oscar Wilde when probing the tortured thoughts of his protagonist Dorian Gray.

But there's nothing cynical about the sentiment: turning failure into a positive experience. Businesses have always had different ways of dealing with disappointments: denial, defensiveness, depersonalization, even discovery in the best of cases.

Not everyone can learn to fail forward, as the leadership consultant John C. Maxwell urged companies to do years ago. It still hurts to own your setbacks. Crawling out from even a small hole of self-pity isn't always easy. Careers are wrecked by a single wrong turn. Few people are able to dissect their humiliations, much less want to do so. And fewer still like to share them—or derive something valuable from the experience.

Anyone who tells you this is easy is either wide-eyed or deceitful. The fear of failure is perhaps the biggest corporate shortcoming of all. GE, at least, is working hard at loosening up. Its failed partnership with Quirky took it places it hadn't been in a very long time, with cool products quickly produced— maybe too quickly. So did its GE Hitachi experiment: trying out an idea on customers before creating it, having the courage to stop the project based on customer reaction, then moving on to something else more promising.

David Kidder has helped GE come a long way by provocatively challenging the company's strategy around innovation, encouraging productive failure, and driving a portfolio approach as a new way to manage growth—backing a large volume of ideas, of which perhaps only one or two will see daylight. And like the philosopher's stone of old, which was fabled to turn base metals into gold, Aarif Aziz has found a way to flip failure into useful, constructive lessons.

## AT THE VERY LEAST, MOVE ON

Recognizing failure isn't something to bury and forget—that seems like a pretty good starting point.

From failure, let's move to the difficult act of success in Chapter 9. The test of a partnership doesn't end with the introduction of a new product or technology. The true measure of success lies in bringing the best ideas, approaches, and lessons of a partnership back into the rest of your organization—and how well or poorly they're embraced and adopted.

# 9

---

# Scaling the Partnership Lessons Across the Enterprise

Things blow up when fear meets reality.

—TIM ARMSTRONG, *CEO of Oath, a division of Verizon*

AT THE END OF CHAPTER 8, I LEFT YOU WITH THE IDEA THAT the real test of a successful partnership is whether it has staying power once you bring elements of it back inside your organization. What's the reception like among veteran leaders, as well as the rank and file? Will the most positive, useful lessons stick, and—more important—will they spread throughout the company? Can the partnership help raise the tolerance for risk, spur innovation, spark quicker decisions, rejuvenate a sclerotic culture, bring the company back to peak performance?

As tough as it is to work through differences with your startup partner, it's *far* more difficult to gain acceptance of your new thinking and approaches among your familiar colleagues. This isn't as counterintuitive as it may sound at first. Inertia is prevalent in established companies.

Chances are your boss, peers, and subordinates have more to lose than any startup you might work with. That's because your fellow employees have so much invested in the status quo—their safe routines, trepidation to stir things up, concerns about jeopardizing their career advancement—even if, over time, it's killing them and the organization.

This chapter is about that fear—and, especially, the creative ways that some legacy companies are overcoming it in order to defeat intransigence from within. That's the only way to bring sunshine into the dark corners of the corporate matrix.

I'd like to foreshadow some of those benefits by sharing some findings from our Global Partnership Study. Mature companies motivated by changing corporate culture in order to be more entrepreneurial are 67 percent more likely to have successful partnerships than those driven by other goals, including adding a new product or service line (62 percent), increasing revenue (60 percent), or acquiring a new technology (50 percent).

Rooting around that subject brings to light another surprising conclusion: enterprises with successful partnerships are nearly three times as likely to experience a strong, positive impact on the rest of the organization, compared with those that had unsuccessful alliances. That's a striking contrast—and a powerful affirmation of the favorable halo effect that rewarding partnerships can have on an entire company.

## DON'T LET FEAR KILL AN AUSPICIOUS PARTNERSHIP

"Things blow up when fear meets reality," says Tim Armstrong, the CEO of Oath, the new division at Verizon that houses AOL and Yahoo brands. He speaks from long experience as both a young entrepreneur and a veteran of Disney, Google, AOL, and its new corporate partner, Verizon. Armstrong truly believes in his team at Oath but is candid about those areas where risk and fear sometimes create road barriers.

To Armstrong's credit, he has promoted a company culture where people are always learning and growing. During our interview, he explained he's applying that maxim to persuade AOL insiders, who, according to Armstrong, have repeatedly stymied a promising partnership with theSkimm. Founded in 2012 by Danielle Weisberg and Carly Zakin, theSkimm shoots a free email newsletter each day—popular stories, quotes of the day, articles other people are following—to four million subscribers. Says Armstrong: "Its news is highly curated, has a lot of personality and character, and a high adoption rate, especially in the demographic that we've been looking to work with"—millennial women. "We have tried multiple times to work with the startup." The plan was to distribute theSkimm, perhaps with the help of the highly popular *Huff Post*, and help monetize it beyond the site's ads and Skimm Ahead, a mobile app that costs $2.99 a month.

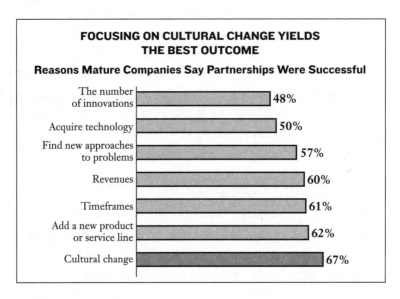

**FOCUSING ON CULTURAL CHANGE YIELDS THE BEST OUTCOME**

**Reasons Mature Companies Say Partnerships Were Successful**

| | |
|---|---|
| The number of innovations | 48% |
| Acquire technology | 50% |
| Find new approaches to problems | 57% |
| Revenues | 60% |
| Timeframes | 61% |
| Add a new product or service line | 62% |
| Cultural change | 67% |

The problem? To Armstrong, it is fear. "I think our teams don't understand the basic building blocks of how theSkimm was built," says Armstrong. "There's the fear on the company side that you may be bringing people in who are actually way more experienced, talented, and focused on an area than you are—'Oh, my goodness, they may take over our roles!' And there's a fear on the startup side, which is, 'This company is so much bigger and so much more sophisticated than us; they may find out that we only know one sliver of this!' "

I've known Armstrong for a long time, since the days of the partnership P&G did with Google that I described in Chapter 1. I got to know him even better during the five years that I served on AOL's board, before the Verizon buyout. I've seen him fired up at board meetings. But on this chilly morning in early April, sitting down with him in his corner office in Manhattan's East Village, I see a sense of frustration, no doubt exacerbated by his punishing calendar.

Just back from Washington, D.C., Armstrong is flopped down in a leather chair that can barely contain his tall frame. "You see the difference in the cultures," he muses. "You have a startup that's obsessive about people, customers—and you have a giant corporation that's supposed to be doing it, but instead people feel like they're caught inside the company." He winces as if in pain. "The leader is trying to drive something, but doesn't have buy-in because of whatever the culture is around the fear-based stuff."

In other words, Armstrong is backing a promising relationship with theSkimm that's perhaps dead on arrival, choked by forces from within.

The same forces can conspire to kill an already completed partnership, even one that has achieved great success by any measure. In the face of critical choices, to say nothing of radical change, human nature can opt for the status quo. "Habit is a great deadener," says one of Samuel Beckett's protagonists in his extraordinary play *Waiting for Godot*.

## DEFUSE THE RESISTANCE WITHIN—AND MOVE FORWARD

Recall from Chapter 7 the partnership between Levi Strauss & Co. and the Seattle startup Evrnu to produce jeans using

98 percent recycled material. LS&Co. and Evrnu have the will and the means to make jeans on a massive scale in a more sustainable fashion—yet it's taking longer than they had expected to get there. Why?

In part it is due to institutional resistance to change. "Product innovation is still a disruptive feature of our business," says Paul Dillinger, LS&Co.'s head of global product innovation. Despite backing from CEO Chip Bergh, there had been sporadic pushback internally as teams worked to figure out the business case and consumer value proposition for something that's never been created before but that the team believed was a big game-changer. "As with any new product innovation, it's not going to have a clear unit of volume or a financial metric behind it—and that makes it hard sometimes to sell the idea internally."

Dillinger was looking for incremental investment to finance the recycled denim project and save even more water in the production process. "Hopefully, we activate this goal and suddenly everyone leans into it," says Dillinger. In the meantime, he says, "we need to learn from our Google partnership: treat each barrier, each setback, as a welcome problem to solve, while not slowing down." Words of wisdom for any legacy company trying to reignite its passion for innovation.

In spring 2017 I once again visited LS&Co.'s headquarters in San Francisco, to reconnect with the LS&Co. players in this book. I wanted to see firsthand if the learning from the Google partnership was scaling across the organization. And I wanted to check in on the status of the budding Evrnu alliance.

Sure enough, the learning from the Google partnership was taking hold: the Levi's team had worked with Evrnu on an incremental budget and project plan, and they are proceeding toward a commercial proof of concept for the technology. As for the lessons of the Google partnership scaling? Levi's brand president, James Curleigh, summed it up: "It's incredible who we are now partnering with. The caliber of our partnerships has changed. Our organization is more adventurous. How we think about innovation is more ambitious."

## DON'T JUST GET BUY-IN FROM THE TOP

Rick Morrison gets a little animated when the subject of selling his wares into larger partners comes up. Morrison is the co-founder and CEO of Comprehend Systems of Redwood City, California, a tech guy trying to make his mark in the pharmaceutical world. It ought to be an easy sell: his cloud-based software makes sense of the scads of data produced by life sciences giants such as Merck, AstraZeneca, and Astellas Pharma, helping them accelerate bringing new medicines and therapies to market by better understanding and managing the rough roads to FDA approval for new drugs.

Morrison is driven by a financial and a personal story. Clinical trials are slow and costly, moving as they do through an ever more rigorous series of randomized and double-blind tests, reviews, and so on before getting an okay from the FDA. Fewer than one in six biologics makes it to the finish line; for cancer drugs, that success rate drops to one in twenty.

Considering that pharmaceutical companies invest $160 billion a year in R&D, anything that can speed the approval process and increase the odds of success—or help jettison early what has little chance of succeeding—may start to put a dent in those costs. That's Comprehend's proposition.

The Redwood City company is focusing on the development of new medicines not just because that's where a lot of the attention and money are but because this is a personal mission for Morrison. His mother successfully battled cancer, so he knows firsthand the impact of therapy breakthroughs. That helps drive his entrepreneurial mission and the company's higher purpose.

Neither of these factors makes his overture to companies any easier. As we have seen with each of the startups we profile in this book, selling a new concept into established enterprises is heavy lifting. From 2009 to 2015, I served on the advisory board of a startup called MarketShare, which offered companies a new predictive-analytics platform to help them spend their marketing budgets more productively. It took us years to gain momentum. We offered a new-to-the-world capability, and managers in mature companies—especially in procurement—did not know how to value us and where we fit in their business processes. A cover story in *Harvard Business Review*, written by our cofounder Wes Nichols, helped us break through—and we sold MarketShare to Neustar in 2015.

Rick Morrison and his purposeful team have the same challenge as MarketShare—especially with the procurement function in established companies. "When we do not fit into their models, some procurement teams at first may not understand us. We are new, we are doing something they have never done before," says Morrison. But he has no problem explaining Comprehend to people at the top, provided he can get to them. "CEOs want to be on the cutting edge. But sometimes there are individuals below who are afraid their career will stall if they try something new and fail. When there is that kind of inertia, it can be a tough sell."

Morrison believes the root cause of the problem lies in incentive structures. "If you're a C-level executive at a Fortune 500 company, you want to show the world quickly that you're innovative, that you can grow the top line," he explains. "Whereas if you're three levels down it may seem more important to grow your career. Innovation is cool, but it's safer to do what worked in the past."

So how do you treat the inertia? Nearly every entrepreneur faces this challenge daily—here is Morrison's advice: "Prove that you can help people with something that they care about. One of their core business issues. Do that, and you can get in there and make buying your product a no-brainer." He adds that once his team breaks through in one division or company, they can gain access to others: "We can get started with a single study team or therapeutic area, add a bigger opportunity area for the company and improve value, and then more teams see it."

The process starts with support from the top but relies on convincing the midlevel folks, who are building their careers, of a tangible benefit. The truth is, shaking up their world a little can give midlevel leaders the means to accelerate their career. I certainly found that in my career—every innovation I embraced as I was working my way up at P&G accelerated my progression. Even the ones that failed.

## TO WIN SKEPTICS OVER TO A NEW IDEA, BREAK A MENTAL PARADIGM—AND SOCIALIZE IT

Over the last few years, Target has had enough come-to-Jesus meetings to fill a multivolume encyclopedia. They finally realized they'd missed the boat on the digital revolution . . . by a decade. A disastrous $2 billion expansion into Canada had to be shuttered in less than two years. And a massive data breach—in which some forty million Target credit and debit card numbers were stolen—forced out CEO Gregg Steinhafel, a thirty-five-year veteran.

That drubbing, that continual humbling, has loosened up Target as an organization, made it a little less self-assured, a little more receptive to experiments. You can see that openness to new approaches most obviously at Open House in downtown San Francisco, the Lucite consumer lab I discussed in Chapter 3, a place where people off the street can try out interconnected smart-home devices, some of which are carried in Target stores. Do they like these gizmos? Are they confused by the idea of the Internet of Things? Target wants to know.

In other words, Target is hacking itself. There's a neat idea.

Only, it turns out, it's not so simple, as I learned by visiting the guy who oversees Open House for Target, Gene Han. Han, who is head of the San Francisco Innovation Center and vice president of Target's consumer Internet of Things, is both a gearhead and a financial analyst—skills that have served him well since he joined Target in 2002. So has his dexterity as a translator, or what he calls "learning different business languages."

A first-generation Korean American, Han was born in Seoul but grew up in Chicago. His dad worked in an auto body shop and his mom was an assembly worker; neither spoke English. Han had to translate for them, starting as a very young kid. At age eight he had to figure out and then explain the U.S. tax code so the family could file their taxes. "I think that's what makes me really effective in terms of working in both worlds," Han says. Sometimes that means straddling the innovative, entrepreneurial world and Target's still somewhat cautious HQ.

Before Open House, Target had CityTarget, which Han helped develop as part of Target's strategy team. The first eighty-thousand-square-foot stores, roughly 60 percent the size of suburban Targets, opened in urban centers including Chicago, Seattle, and L.A. back in 2012. My daughter was a student at UCLA at the time, and CityTarget opened in her neighborhood. I saw firsthand how much the store concept appealed to a millennial; she shopped in the store nearly every day.

In retrospect, the concept seems obvious. But at first it wasn't—at least, not to Target higher-ups. "I can't tell you the number of people that told me, generally not to my face, 'It'll never work, *never* work,'" Han recalls.

Drawing on sales data from urban versions of Whole Foods,

Walgreens, and J.C. Penney, Han created a proxy for the sales metrics. "Once I brought the analytics to bear, showed people the dollars per square foot, it started to alleviate concerns," he recalls.

Next, Han and his team built several prototypes of a City-Target store to test the concept and help Target leaders visualize what the store would look like.

"Having a place where people can build is *really* important," Han stresses, as is being able to demonstrate your idea to skeptics. "You have to have people see it to really understand. You can't ask them to envision it on a piece of paper." And you have to exercise a little strategic cunning. "The closer the ideas get to the core, the more you need to socialize, bring people on board," explains Han.

## CREATE BIG CHANGES IN SMALL INCREMENTS

Rick Dalzell, whom you met in Chapter 8, came to Amazon in 1997 and served as its CIO until he left in 2007. Dalzell neatly summarizes the philosophy of Jeff Bezos, "We are in business to innovate on behalf of the customer." But because customers rarely know what they want until they see it, as Steve Jobs famously postulated, "our job was to figure it out," says Dalzell. "It meant we made a significant amount of mistakes along the way." Not only that, but the abundant innovators at Amazon also had to deal with resistance from some people within Amazon, whose duty it was to keep the fast-moving enterprise running well. Dalzell reflects on how Amazon managed the risk and the naysayers. "We were set up to run in small teams and do low-cost experiments to determine what customer innovations would work."

One example: Super Saver Shipping, better known today as Amazon Prime. Greg Greeley, the leader of financial planning and analysis, wanted to know just how significant fast (and free) shipping was to customers. Was it more or less important than selection and prices of books (Amazon's main offering then)? "Some on the finance team and other corners of the company thought it was a crazy idea," Dalzell recalls. How could you justify and support what appeared to be a completely unnecessary cost? But multiple small tests convinced management that fast, free shipping really mattered to customers. "It moved the needle—and turned out to be one of the most important programs at Amazon."

Why was free shipping so resonant with people? It removed a critical friction point for consumers: people started to buy more things, and so Prime began paying for itself. And it created perhaps the most powerful virtuous cycle at Amazon: it eventually allowed the company to deliver more free benefits to more customers—things like unlimited Kindle reading and access to Kindle's lending library, and unlimited streaming of Amazon's growing video content in competition with Netflix.

Dalzell cites using a similar approach of taking small steps in the recent test of Amazon Go, its convenience store that lets you enter via an app, scan things like snacks and drinks, and exit without stopping at a cashier. "Point of sale is no longer a blocker," says Dalzell, just as it's not an issue in using Uber and Lyft. He expects to see many more incremental improvements from Amazon and others that make buying a nearly frictionless experience.

Dalzell was one of the key people in building Amazon's e-commerce platform and its personalization engine, which recommends new book titles based on a customer's previous shopping history. He had a similar impact on Walmart. As VP of information systems for seven years, he helped to advance its transformative data warehousing strategy, allowing the retailer's suppliers to tap into its demographic sales information to see what was selling and what was not, and automatically refill shelves. "It was a perpetual inventory system in all the stores, facilitating automatic replenishment without a buyer or a person in the store having to submit an order," explains Dalzell in a light Kentucky drawl.

At the beginning, the concept of store-level automatic replenishment had little support. "The store managers and their local teams struggled with it," he remembers. "They couldn't believe a computer could do a better job than a human. None of the regional VPs or store managers dared to surrender control of replenishment." So the development team found a champion in a tech-savvy Walmart buyer who wanted to try out the new system just for car batteries in the winter season. "We showed it in 10 percent of the stores. He did all the work for us; it wouldn't have been successful if we forced the system on the buyers." The sell-through rate was better than ever, and ultimately adopted across all replenishable inventory at Walmart stores.

The core lesson when it comes to big new things? "Break it down into small bite-sized chunks," says Dalzell. "Demonstrate that it works and push it across different categories."

## CREATE SOMETHING NEW—AND SELL IT BY *SHOWING* IT

Here's another approach to overcoming corporate negativity: "How do you disrupt yourself in a way that doesn't screw up your current revenue streams, but allows you to get some bandwidth to invest in new capabilities and new market opportunities?"

The question comes from Zackery Hicks, chief information officer of Toyota Motor North America. He's also the CEO of Toyota Connected, a new unit focused on using data analytics to develop new ideas and products for consumers, dealers, businesses, and governments. Connected isn't just about cloud-based software to link different functions and devices in a vehicle in order to turn it into a smartphone on wheels. It is also modeling how individuals actually drive and coming up with new pricing models for insurance, providing real-time road information that drivers can share with other commuters to avoid accidents, and partnering with lots of startups. The idea is to expand "mobility" way beyond cars, including helping disabled and blind people get around better. Hicks, to put a fine point on it, is exploding the idea of what an automobile is.

But it's been a near-epic struggle.

His quest to shake up Toyota began in the eye of a double storm. First came the Great Recession in 2008. Auto sales plunged 15.4 percent year over year, the worst totals since 1992. Everyone was looking to slash costs, not create something new. Months later, a spiraling crisis hit the company. It started with reported problems with floor mats, then accelerator pedals, followed by complaints about electronic throttle systems and brakes.

By the end, Toyota had to recall 2.3 million vehicles. Hicks himself was recalled to IT from administrative services and brought back as CIO. "Our call centers became overwhelmed and couldn't handle the volume," he remembers. "Then you had all those people showing up at the dealerships with claims and warranty parts our systems weren't designed to handle. One by one, all the systems began to break."

But why waste a good crisis? Hicks started sorting through the rubble at the back end of a way-overloaded mainframe system. Meantime, Congress, joining with angry consumers, accused the carmaker of hiding the worst. But, as Hicks discovered, there were big discrepancies between problems reported by the press and actual ones in Toyota's database. Hicks was wrestling with the question of when and how data becomes knowledge. Leveraging a recent investment in an emerging big-data tool, Hicks and team drew on disparate internal data sets—from customers, call centers, and warranty claims, along with those from complaints to the National Highway Traffic Safety Administration, among other sources. The media were pushing one narrative; the data sets told another story. But when Hicks took those issues to his quality control department, they said to him, "We don't have time for an IT project."

So Hicks brought the problem to James E. Lentz, CEO of Toyota Motor North America, who had just returned from a Senate hearing—more like a drubbing. "I said, 'Jim, I know our world's on fire, but you gotta give me ten minutes to show you this.' And after I showed it to him he said, 'I want everybody that reports to me to see this.' And that was the game changer."

His argument was that clear data and analytics could help winch Toyota out of the mess. But Hicks still had a fight on his hands. "My own IT team didn't want to do this because it wasn't a traditional way to use data," he remembers. Still, after the recall crisis, the new tool helped convince government officials that Toyota did have appropriate insight into its own internal data. And today that same tool is providing a wide range of insights, from picking up customer complaints on social media to ingesting manufacturing data and predicting when critical machinery is going to fail before it impacts the assembly line.

## HELP CHANGE-RELUCTANT CONSTITUENTS BY EMPOWERING THEM

Hicks demonstrated the benefits on several fronts, offering naysayers not just useful ideas but something new: power. "I started saying, 'Okay, you've got no governance—I'm going to give you the money and the freedom to build this stuff.'" Hicks also began to talk about the need to unlock data from the clutches of IT and siloed business units and democratize it, spreading it around the entire company. "Most new business opportunities impact the whole enterprise," he reasons. He showed the head of Lexus Marketing the beauty of social media combined with predictive analytics—a combination the executive had initially found intrusive. "I said I can predict when a customer is going to defect," Hicks recalls, illustrating his point with the case of someone who'd bought ten cars from Toyota, complained about his air-conditioning, then visited two Honda dealerships for a new car.

Hicks brought the same persuasive case for matching customer sentiment analysis and social media to Greg Penske, who oversees the second-largest dealership by units sold and leased. Penske couldn't believe what he saw. Other dealerships soon followed. A new idea, Hicks says, "has to be more than just *talk*. For me, a lot of it was just demonstrating capability."

Proof that something novel actually works—that's what disbelievers need in order to win them over.

## ENCOURAGE EMPLOYEES TO CONTRIBUTE THEIR IDEAS

Zackery Hicks says that a lot of employees have great things to contribute but never go public with them because no one ever asks them for their ideas. That's why he created a one-day annual event called Toyota Innovation Fair. It encourages teams across the company to compete for prizes and funding by building prototypes that address current challenges or push the carmaker in new directions. The judges include a couple of group vice presidents and general managers.

But unlike the "Startup Challenge" competitions for Motorola Solutions employees (Chapter 3), Toyota's fair also invites various vendor partners—including Cognizant, Amazon, Infosys, and Microsoft—as well as outsiders like Zappos and Intel Capital to present some of their latest insights and technologies.

The results of these employee-developed innovations are both big (new ways to sell used cars) and small (a lunch-delivery app), and that's just fine with Hicks and his team.

Spreading data analytics, uncorking employee innovations, and bringing in leading thinkers and doers from the outside has "changed the conversation inside," says Hicks.

## IF YOU'VE BREACHED THE WALL OF RESISTANCE, KNOCK IT DOWN WITH SOMETHING COMPLETELY NEW

Hicks, who combines a boyish-looking charm with a geeky salesperson's bluntness, parlayed his triumphs over the innovation resistors into the creation of an entirely new company within Toyota—and moved it far from the madding crowd to Preston Hollow, a neighborhood in north Dallas, Texas. Launched in early 2016, Toyota Connected is about "customer experience and mobility, however the customer describes that," says Hicks.

Some of that intellectual power is devoted to connecting all the automotive electronics in the cloud. But Hicks is also pushing extravehicular developments. Project BLAID, for example, is a partnership with the carmaker's Robot Group to work on providing a hands-free wearable device to help the blind and visually impaired navigate indoor areas including homes, offices, malls, and airports. Relying on cameras to detect features and communicate them via speakers and vibration, it can discern objects such as signs for exits, bathrooms, and storefronts, as well as stairs and escalators (and, one day, object and facial recognition).

Toyota Connected is also partnering with DEKA, the R&D factory of Dean Kamen, who created the sometimes hailed and often pilloried Segway personal transporter. DEKA is developing a new version of the iBOT, the electric wheelchair with two sets of wheels that allows disabled folks to rise from sitting to a standing posture and "walk" up and down stairs. The wheelchair will also be able to maneuver around rough terrain such as dirt roads. "Toyota is the largest investor in robotics in the world," says Hicks. "A lot of that is around helping the elderly or people with limited mobility have access to it in the future."

All that prep work of wearing down insider resistance has given Hicks permission to work on some truly outlier ideas. But he's keenly aware of the fragility of his efforts, given that corporate innovation resistance can reassert itself. "Your old processes will kill you," he muses. "I think that's why you see old companies and investors buying Silicon Valley startups. These large companies' bureaucracy and weight can just crush the innovation, which is the reason they bought them in the first place."

## TO CHANGE YOUR CULTURE, START SOMETHING NEW WITHIN

IBM, the company that brought you Watson, has also developed within IBM a burgeoning startup that is helping to reshape a culture of innovation inside the tech giant, as well as at client companies. IBM Bluemix Garage, as it's called, is a curious hybrid. While it falls within the species of consultancy, it's way more than that. Its first obligation is to help clients big and small adapt to and make use of Bluemix, IBM's developer platform on the IBM cloud. The platform runs millions of complicated applications, such as a program that lets callers talk directly with customer-service reps or one that allows employees to engage in outreach via LinkedIn to attract new talent. Bluemix gives clients' software developers an easy-to-use system without having to deal with difficult infrastructure or hosting; they can just write code to their hearts' content.

Beyond that, the Garage is a link between enterprises and startups. The little guys get access to big brothers and sisters, and large companies get turned on to innovative entrepreneurs. That's easy in the San Francisco Garage, which is neighbor to twenty-five very young companies in the same building. IBM occupies a couple of floors with a lot of open workspaces, as you would find in most any startup, and a sight you would never have seen just a few years ago at Big Blue: dozens of Apple laptops, everyone's standard workhorse at the Garage.

"We're a consultancy within a large company, which would normally be known as professional services," says John Phelan, a practice leader who oversees the inaugural Garage in San Francisco (there are similar operations in London, Nice, Toronto, New York, Melbourne, Singapore, and Tokyo). "But we're also like a startup, transforming businesses." Adds Sarah Plantenberg, a senior designer who is Phelan's number two: "Our mission is not to be a lab services arm for our clients, but to teach them how to transform themselves, learning practices and techniques we use that have helped us be successful."

The Garage's tacit, but no less critical, assignment is to break down a client's resistance to change. "It's really about how the client company can innovate within itself," says Phelan. Sometimes the Garage just tries to help corporate clients become leaner and faster by bridging the chasm, say, between the IT department and business development, getting the groups to talk to each other and to stop pulling in different directions.

In one case, the Garage had to sign a nondisclosure agreement with a small group within a larger client not to blab to that company at large. Why? The unit wanted to develop something new with Garage team help and stress-test it before letting the rest of the company in on it—a preemptive strike on cynicism.

Whatever the push, the Garage mantra is to take it one mincing step at a time. "We say it over and over in here: 'What is the simplest thing that could work for this code or for this client?'

or whatever," says Marlena Compton, a Garage developer—and one of a motley team of men and women, mostly young, of every size, shape, ethnicity, and race.

How has the Garage pushed IBM?

PHELAN: "Well, it's—"

PLANTENBERG: "It's positioned IBM in a much broader context and an understanding because—"

PHELAN: "Like a business- and user-centric context as opposed to just a technology platform—"

PLANTENBERG: "IBM always had an end-user-centered focus, but I think what we are bringing to the Bluemix table is where it fits in the culture and understanding of those larger companies."

In other words, the Garage is helping IBM understand how to bring not just product innovation to clients but process change as well.

These two high-voltage executives have worked together since 2011, and they often finish—or interrupt—each other's sentences. Phelan, an ardent downhill skier in his late fifties, is the more low-key of the two; his amused smile seems to hide things he has thought better of sharing. Plantenberg is tall, slim, in her mid-forties, and wearing Princess Leia–style braids on the day of my visit; she's all kinetic energy and holds back nothing. "We're part of IBM, but we're also part of a change, a catalytic change overall in IBM," she philosophizes.

But how, exactly? Phelan explains, using an analogy that he typically draws on to illustrate how the Garage works with clients: negotiating a path through Grand Central Station at rush hour to get to the clock in the center of the crowded station. "You don't predefine each way you're going to maneuver because it's impossible to anticipate all the people walking across," he says. "I'm meandering and adapting and pivoting, but I also know there's a clock, and that's where I'm headed."

What works for their clients may also work within your own walls. Set a goal—whether it's changing the idea of customer service or creating more of an innovative culture—and strive to work your way through. "It's a process," says Kelly Bailey, a senior designer at the Bluemix Garage who has since moved to a job at Visa. "A way to create change over time."

## WHEN ALL ELSE FAILS, REBUILD THE COMPANY AS A SERIES OF ENTREPRENEURIAL FIEFS—SEPARATE BUT UNDER ONE FLAG

It sounds crazy, maybe even suicidal.

But it's essentially what CEO Flemming Ørnskov has done with Shire—in just three years, and with irrefutable success. True, Shire is an $11 billion (in sales) company sharply focused on rare diseases, not a $125 billion industrial colossus like GE. Still, it's a model worth looking at. Getting there in such a short time has tested all the strategic, tactical, and social skills of this Danish physician who trained in pediatrics and then went on to get an MBA from INSEAD and a master's in public health from Harvard University. (Disclosure: Shire has been a client of my company.)

"I was basically inheriting a company where the future was highly in question," says Ørnskov, whose fluent English has a slight Scandinavian accent. Some of Shire's patents were about to expire, competitive perils were arising, and new technologies threatened to overtake the company. Founded in 1986 by four Brits, Shire lurched its way into the twenty-first century by acquiring a hodgepodge of other biopharma companies that produced drugs to treat, for example, attention deficit hyperactivity disorder (ADHD), gastrointestinal diseases, and infections caused by hepatitis C and the herpes virus.

To get a feel for how the company had evolved, Ørnskov talked to as many former executives as he could track down, as well as leaders from other competitors. He liked some of what he learned, but wanted to build it out bigger and faster. "My idea was that Shire could become the partner of choice, the acquirer of choice, and that by agglomerating all these companies we could build scale and scope and reach." But he would do so systematically, accumulating a full complement of companies that focused on rare diseases and, at the same time, reorganizing the way Shire functioned from the inside.

Ørnskov was creating a new kind of company—capable of expanding to virtually any size but entrepreneurial at its core and, as a result, an oasis of protected and well-funded innovative efforts. From a nurturing center, new ideas and new products would constantly sprout like new blood vessels: angiogenesis in a corporate setting.

The inspiration for this model came from the years Ørnskov spent at Children's Hospital in Copenhagen. "I saw the opportunity to take all the distinct diseases and rare diseases that affect different organs and make a company out of it," he says. Strolling through Shire now is a bit like walking through the various departments of a hospital, "whether it's transplantation, immunology, hematology, ophthalmology, oncology—dealing with specific patient needs, but all within the same house."

Today, he says, "Shire is a conglomeration of a bunch of companies that got together and have a cohesive entrepreneurial culture. Most people at Shire don't perceive it as one big company; each of the franchises sees themselves as startups." In three-plus years, Ørnskov has acquired more than ten companies, partnered with fistfuls of other startups, increased sales from $5 billion to $11 billion, expanded to 24,000 people from 5,000, and nearly tripled the company's market capitalization, to more than $50 billion. It serves patients in more than one hundred countries around the globe and has operations in sixty-eight.

To get to that point, Ørnskov has had to beat back disbelievers not just among financial analysts but also within Shire. "First, I had to persuade my board that such a strategy could work," says Ørnskov, who is tall and athletic, with a passion for soccer. He'd had a series of dress rehearsals for that boardroom performance while doing executive-level work at Ikaria (therapeutics for critical care), Life-Cycle Pharma (a Danish firm now known as Veloxis Pharmaceuticals A/S), Bausch & Lomb, and Bayer.

For Shire's board, CEO Ørnskov sketched out the universe of what amounted to a cottage industry: fifty to a hundred small rare-disease companies, each with a particular molecule or focus, out of which perhaps one or two broke through with something big every couple of years. "By partnering with or acquiring these small companies, every second year we could probably pick up a company that might grow to the size of $5 billion or $6 billion." Following that strategy, he argued, "we could build a sustainable, double-digit-growth business that we could build around the world, fund out of cash flow, and drive profitability."

## REFOCUS RELUCTANT EMPLOYEES BY GIVING THEM NEW RESPONSIBILITIES

Since the financial projections seemed to make sense, the board was a relatively easy sell. But among company employees, not so much. "There were a lot of people in the organization that had this 'not-invented-here' mentality," Ørnskov recalls, especially given the radical overhaul he was pushing.

Ground zero for the shakeup was R&D, the lab-bench types who were pursuing scientific advancement in time-honored but outdated ways. Ørnskov killed its research committee, subbing in a pipeline committee, half of whose members would pursue regular R&D activities while the other half chased external opportunities—that is, candidates for partnerships or acquisition.

This was all part of Ørnskov's "franchise" model to redirect a lot of Shire's efforts toward innovation and faster product development. He created more than a half-dozen units in different areas—including genetic diseases, immunology, and hematology—each overseen by commercial and R&D leaders. "If it's an early-stage incubator situation, where they talk about getting the product approved or licensing a new product, they do that in the pipeline committee," Ørnskov explains. "If it's more about the commercial execution, they go to the in-line committee and we discuss it there." To relieve scientists of most bureaucratic chores, Ørnskov consolidated groups such as finance, human resources, and information technology into a global service organization. In essence, he allowed them to go forth and act like incubators.

## LEAVE STARTUPS IN THEIR OWN HABITATS AS LONG AS POSSIBLE

The third group Ørnskov had to persuade consisted of potential partners. Why, in the name of Asclepius, would they want to pair up with—or, worse, be acquired by—Shire, which was just going to swallow them up?

Having worked in both large and small companies, Ørnskov was sympathetic to those fears and developed an intriguing approach to integration. "In most cases, we would let them run loose for another one to three years, just to see how things went and not stop any great research," he says, before bringing them into the fold, giving most of them space among the other franchises in Cambridge, Massachusetts, Shire's U.S. headquarters. And even then, he would have them report directly to him.

"We wanted to give them a feeling of being a small company, a startup, within Shire," says Ørnskov. Every partner, every acquisition is on a different timetable for that integration, so that the best work of each company can play out to an optimal conclusion. Even for acquired companies, this is a radically different approach compared to the usual M&A aftermath.

For the most part, the model is working. Ørnskov's latest insight is to organize his franchises—those commercial and R&D units—into downtown clusters in most of the different countries in which Shire operates. That not only perpetuates the feel of working at a startup, it also fosters creativity. "People who are solving problems together should sit together," he says. Like the chiefs of GE and Motorola Solutions, Ørnskov believes that moving operations from the suburbs to the center of cities puts his company closer to the nerve center of new things and great energetic talent.

PARTNERSHIP SUCCESS is ultimately about breeding *more* successes. Remember the halo effect that good partnerships can have on entire enterprises, underscored by the Global Partnership Study, noted at the beginning of the book. That virtuous cycle involves transplanting the best things in your relationship with a startup into your own organization and allowing some of that young and vibrant RNA to direct the act of rebuilding within. That often requires scaling or cracking the walls of resistance, the years of defensive fortification that every legacy company has allowed to build up.

In this chapter, we've seen different approaches to beating back institutional resistance to new ideas and to new ways of doing things. AOL has been grappling with the collective fear of outsiders coming inside; Levi Strauss & Co. has been trying to diffuse the resistance within to disruptive innovation. In very different ways, Comprehend Systems and Toyota have demonstrated proof of various concepts to overcome inertia and pushback. IBM has taken an unbuttoned approach by moving ahead in different ways to change people's minds. At Shire, the CEO has built a new structure that is all but impervious to the enemies of innovation.

When it comes to FastWorks, its dramatic and years-long process of self-overhaul, GE hopes that everyone will embrace the changes. "We're not forcing anybody to do anything," says Viv Goldstein, GE's global director of innovation acceleration. "But you're always going to get people that don't want to change. It's just the way they are. At some stage, this isn't going to be the company they want to work for. If it's not a good fit, we'll encourage them to move on."

If you're going to build the kind of company where one success breeds many others, you have to do more than just convince ensconced pessimists. Sparking and spreading the changes wrought by a successful partnership demands great leadership of a particular kind that includes a willingness to cultivate and support disciples who themselves become leaders.

That's the subject of Chapter 10.

# 10

# New Leadership Wanted: Outsiders on the Inside

You need a radical outsider to help you do it.

—David Kidder, *CEO, Bionic*

I N 2013, Beth Comstock, GE's vice chair who heads up innovation, marketing, and communications, asked David Kidder to address the company's annual leadership conference in Boca Raton, Florida. Kidder, you'll recall from Chapter 8, is a cofounder of Bionic—a growth solution for large enterprises. At that point, Bionic didn't exist, and while Kidder knew Comstock well, he was a complete stranger to GE.

Comstock invited Kidder to come up onstage and, in front of an audience of GE's global officers, pose a question to GE CEO Jeff Immelt. Kidder, who is something of a mischief maker, eagerly welcomed the challenge.

"I'd never met Jeff in my life, and so I yelled down at him in the front row, 'Jeff, how many $50 million companies did you launch last year?'" Kidder recalls. "I said, 'I'll bet the answer is zero. And if that's actually true, I'd be totally terrified—like, how's it possible with thousands of employees and $90 billion in the bank it doesn't happen, like, *all* the time?'" The auditorium got so quiet you could've heard an LED bulb fail. "Beth breaks this shocking moment and she's like, 'Tell us how you really feel!' And everybody starts to laugh nervously."

After Kidder left the stage, Immelt approached him. Instead

of upbraiding the guest speaker, he embraced him. "He says, 'That was awesome; you're going to come fix this,'" Kidder remembers. "And he goes back onstage and closes the conference by saying, 'That's the most important question in thirty-seven years of this leadership conference.'"

FastWorks, spurred by Lean Startup founder Eric Ries, launched soon after, as did GE's investment portfolio approach to an innovative future, Kidder's contribution. "Jeff knew he needed to change the entire soul of the company and he's done that with Beth," Kidder says. "But you need a radical outsider to help you do it."

Bringing in a radical outsider to change the soul of the company is a jarring thought. Think of archetypal heroes who save a community from calamity—Beowulf, for example, who rescues a Swedish kingdom by slaying the monster Grendel and Grendel's mother, or Shane, the gunslinger who rides into town to defend Wyoming homesteaders from an evil cattle baron. Moses, Jesus, Mohammed, and Buddha were all outsiders to some extent. For our purposes, it's useful to think of outsiders in the literal sense, as people who come from another place—and have a different habit of mind or a more outward-facing view of the world that can help change how things are done within an organization.

The outsider is central to the idea of new leadership. How? It takes a determined and courageous disrupter to dislodge a troubled legacy company from its worst habits and set it on the difficult course of rejuvenation, often by embracing partnerships with startups. "Somebody's got to go to the top of the mountain and tell people, 'This is how we're going to drive growth'—otherwise it's not going to happen," explains Gene Han at Target. It implies different uses of power, inspiration, and influence, and the ability to wield new skills in novel ways.

Outsiders, whether they actually come from another com-

pany or serve as longtime insiders who continually see and agi-
tate for new directions, can be the most effective champions of
positive change.

This new breed of leaders has little swagger and a lot of humility, awed as they often are by the challenges ahead. They
recognize that no one has all the answers; that makes them
eager to learn from other people, particularly those who are
very different from them—folks like entrepreneurs. They know
how to listen and how to delegate, and that inspires trust among
subordinates and allows disciples (and future leaders) to emerge
from the shadows in order to challenge existing circumstances
and offer different solutions.

If leaders can depend on others to do some of the things that
they used to reserve for themselves, they can free up their time
for other activities, such as meeting new people on the outside.
That, in turn, exposes them to new ways of doing things, lessons and ideas they can bring back inside. It's a constant act of
replenishing—and one of the most vital activities of these new-
breed leaders who are outsiders at heart if not in fact.

As it turns out, several of the CEOs of companies you've been
reading about are pure outsiders. Brian Cornell led Safeway, Michael's, Sam's Club, and a division of PepsiCo before coming
to Target in 2014. Flemming Ørnskov started out in academic
medicine before joining various pharmaceutical companies and
taking over as chief of Shire in 2013. And Chip Bergh, Levi
Strauss's CEO since 2011, spent twenty-eight years at Procter
& Gamble.

Then there are insiders who think and act like outsiders.
Ginni Rometty has been at IBM since 1981 (and CEO since
2012) but has long been something of an inside agitator, pushing Big Blue into big new businesses such as consulting, cloud
computing and analytics, and now Watson. Jeff Immelt is also
a lifer, having joined GE in 1982, though he is imbued with a

radical reformer's spirit, having spent the last few years shedding billions of dollars' worth of traditional businesses including plastics, appliances, and finance, welcomed outsiders such as David Kidder and Eric Ries, and played first mover on behalf of FastWorks.

Greg Brown first arrived at Motorola in 2003; in 2008, he became CEO and leveraged the 2011 breakup to reengineer Motorola Solutions, giving new authority to his management team and turning what had been an insular company into a host for ideas and people from the outside.

In Chapter 9 I introduced you to Zack Hicks, the CIO of Toyota Motor North America, who has banged the drum on behalf of change and innovation during his two decades at the automaker, most recently as the CEO of Toyota Connected, which he founded in 2016. "This is one of the few times Toyota has launched a new company headquartered outside of Japan—and has put a non-Japanese person at the head of it," he says.

Before that startup, Hicks worked hard to drive a lot of Toyota's operations and communications to the cloud at a time when everyone was still using Lotus Notes. "I had the parent company saying, 'Hey, you can't do that, you can't put email in the cloud, it's too risky.'" But Hicks had already cut a deal with Microsoft on behalf of Toyota's global president, Akio Toyoda, the founder's grandson. "I leveraged that and it forced the rest of Toyota to do it."

Hicks had found an advocate in Toyoda after his drive to open big data and predictive analytics to everyone in the company. "At that point Akio said, 'I will build the tunnel halfway to you and you build the tunnel halfway to me and we will meet in the middle.' And he's like, 'We gotta dig through this middle bureaucracy.'" Another outsider on the inside.

## BREAK THE RULES, BUT BE CAREFUL HOW FAR YOU PUSH THE LIMITS

Outsiders are generally a healthy elixir for disabled organizations. Except when they try to do too much, too quickly.

Perhaps no one embodies that hazard more colorfully than Durk Jager, the shortest-serving CEO in the history of my alma mater Procter & Gamble (September 1999–July 2000), sandwiched between John Pepper and A.G. Lafley.

Though Durk first joined P&G in 1970, he was always something of an outlander. Growing up in Holland (in farming country, not Amsterdam), he began his career in Europe and broke into higher executive ranks after taking an assignment in Japan, where P&G had failed for years. He not only made a success of a bad situation, he went all in on Japanese culture, learning the language and the rituals of doing business there.

By the time he returned to the United States and became CEO, Jager was bursting with new ideas. Within a couple of months he made available to anyone P&G's twenty-five thousand patents, only 10 percent of which were utilized by its brands. The idea was to pressure everyone on the inside to come up with new products, defying a culture that long prided itself on its internal innovation process. He put more responsibility into the hands of new business managers—all with the intention of driving faster decisions and compressing the product development cycle.

That resulted in a record harvest of successful new brands, such as Febreze and Swiffer. Durk also pushed P&Gers to look outside the company for inspiration, laying the foundations for the Connect and Develop program, which is today an active outreach for partnerships in new products, technology, e-commerce, and supply chain innovations. He even waded into the Internet, an early foray, via Reflect.com, an online retailer of health and beauty products that P&G shut down in 2005, once it had its hands full with the Gillette acquisition.

How could a guy like that fail? It wasn't his drive; Durk truly valued innovation. It wasn't a lack of communication skills. Despite a thick accent, he spoke and wrote English gracefully.

I fondly remember his visit with me and my team in Prague during the summer of 1996, when he was P&G's president. (At the time, I was P&G's general manager of the Czech and Slovak Republics.) Our meeting went hours overtime, and he was charming and fully engaged. At dinner that evening with my group, he spoke eloquently and sincerely about the company, our roles, and the impact we were having.

If anything, Jager was too much of an iconoclast. His impatience pushed him to move fast, perhaps too quickly—and in the process he broke some things. Noticing the up-and-down pricing in packaged goods and the prevalence of inefficient coupons, he decided simply to drop the price of products and sharply reduce temporary price reductions . . . and the business suffered. He had underestimated the impact of merchandising and coupons on creating buzz around brands with retailers and consumers.

P&G's results stumbled in a few consecutive quarters, frustrating Wall Street. A highly ambitious three-way deal with Warner-Lambert and American Home Products unraveled after word leaked out and investors balked at the offering price. As Warner retreated into the hostile clutches of Pfizer, Jager got the blame for the collapse of the proposed deal and P&G's stock plunged 7 percent.

In all those cases of too much too quickly, Durk failed to build full support for his bold agenda. He did not adequately prepare investors for a long and bumpy ride that potentially could bring them to share-price Wonderland. He didn't fully secure the skeptics within P&G. And he did not do enough to create more mini-Durks, a coalition of enthusiasts who could help propagate his work and lead the company into the twenty-first century. P&G's results would dip before rising again with A.G. Lafley, who guided the company through a very successful run in the 2000s.

## INVITE THE BARBARIANS IN

Investor Carl Icahn has made himself an unwelcome guest at a lot of companies over the years. In the early days, he stalked companies such as RJR Nabisco, Texaco, and TWA, which had the same response to Icahn as field mice do to the shadow of a hawk. To defend themselves, they'd invoke so-called poison pills (often to dilute the value of the raider's shares), but Icahn usually walked away with a handsome profit by selling his stock back to the company.

In recent years, Icahn reinvented himself as an activist investor with broader aims to gain board seats in order to restructure companies and unlock suppressed shareholder value. With those goals in mind, he has stalked the likes of Apple, Biogen, Time Warner, and Yahoo. And he pursued no target more persistently than Motorola.

He began acquiring shares in the company in 2007, when Motorola was felled by a plunge in stock price and market share, and on it's way to losing billions of dollars. Icahn sued the company, insisting that it sell its drooping cellphone business. But Greg Brown, who took the helm in 2008 as CEO, didn't act defensively the way a lot of CEOs might have: he encouraged two of Icahn's allies to join the board—and he moved forward with a breakup plan. Only the Great Recession delayed the plan from happening sooner. The split, into Motorola Solutions and

Motorola Mobility, took place in early 2011. Months later, Mobility was sold to Google. And by early 2012, Motorola Solutions had bought back Icahn's stock.

Does Brown feel bitter? Not in the least. "Carl Icahn was instrumental at successfully ensuring the company split up," he says. "It was management's recommendation, but having him as a partner to keep accountability with both management and the board to follow through was very, very important. Having an activist in our stock and boardroom provided a further set of catalysts around urgency and change."

For most of his tenure as CEO, Brown has had activists on his board—and dealt with them in a strikingly nonconfrontational way. "One of the things I consciously did was use their presence constructively to further accelerate the pace of change."

As Icahn and his two allies headed out the door, in came ValueAct Capital Management of San Francisco, a kinder and gentler activist, which upped its 5.9 percent ownership to an uncontested 10 percent. Brown welcomed the group as an ally.

"ValueAct had a different thesis," he recalls. "Icahn successfully split Motorola. ValueAct worked with me in further refining Motorola Solutions, trimming down the assets to where we have the gem I always believed we were when I joined the company." He cites specifically the investor's help in providing focus, jettisoning businesses that weren't competitive, and supporting efforts at capital efficiency. "ValueAct was given any and all forms of information about our company so they could sit at the table with us, challenge management, and push us to get the information we needed to run the business better," Brown points out. "Now, that's not for the faint of heart."

In fact, it emboldened Brown to invite a $1 billion investment from venture capitalist firm Silver Lake Partners of Menlo Park, California, in 2015, just as ValueAct was slimming its ownership to 8 percent. Brown regarded Silver Lake, which backs rising young Silicon Valley stars, as the key to forming new partnerships with entrepreneurs. "I said, 'Let's invite them in, and while we don't necessarily need the capital, let's take advantage of Silver Lake's technology orientation, their location on Sand Hill Road, their insights in broader deal-making, and think of them as virtual business development or M&A,'" Brown explains. "Let's use Silver Lake as an extension and an accelerant into our CTO group and M&A. And they have two seats in our boardroom. And people are like, 'My God, why did you give them two board seats?' And the answer is, 'Because we couldn't give them three.'"

Consider the implications. Greg Brown didn't summon these "barbarians," as Bryan Burrough and John Helyar famously called corporate raiders in their 1989 classic business book. But once they were at his gate, Brown invited them in as guests, learned from their experience, perspectives, and agenda, and—most critically—leveraged the commotion they created to launch the transformations at the company that he wanted and needed to make.

If Icahn enabled the Motorola breakup and ValueAct helped clarify Motorola Solutions' mission, Silver Lake turned the company toward the outside into new partnerships and acquisitions in such areas as augmented virtual reality, command-center software, the Internet of Things, and data capture and analytics. "Those are things not 'natural' to what we do at Motorola Solutions because of our heritage as more of a hardware company or a platform company, and we need the speed of development and the focus of entrepreneurs to be integrated into our cycle of innovation in such a way that one plus one equals three," says Brown. As a result, he claims, Motorola Solutions is today becoming more of a software and services company.

## EMPOWER AMBASSADORS TO LEAD THE CHANGES INSIDE YOUR COMPANY

While Motorola was still in turmoil, Brown sought to remake his new company in an unusual way: by giving up some control to subordinates.

I've known Greg since I sat on the board of Motorola from 2005 to 2011 and served on the compensation and leadership committees. He's a broad-shouldered guy, with an open and friendly face—bespectacled, framed by a white-and-gray comb-back—someone you might easily mistake for a college athletic coach. While he's in the business of communications technology, he passionately believes in personal interaction. His quiet baritone and unruffled temperament make him exceedingly accessible, as his management team is keenly aware.

Eduardo Conrado, the chief innovation and strategy officer I introduced earlier, didn't hesitate to approach him a couple of years ago with some sharp criticism. His complaint centered on something as mundane as the monthly management meetings. But it touched on just about every vital issue and challenge facing Motorola Solutions, including Brown's role. "Eduardo said, 'Look, you've made a lot of good changes, Greg, but we're still looking at the business too traditionally. We have these monthly CEO ops reviews and in them you drill down in detail, but you do it on the traditional lens of the business: product sales, backlogs, competition. And people report out. But we're not thinking about it right. You should think about using your time differently.' This was hugely powerful."

It turned out that executives spent a lot of time preparing for the monthly meeting, creating and repackaging a lot of existing material just for Brown's consumption. Greg hadn't even been aware of it. "I said, 'No more. We're still gonna have CEO ops for a half day, but *you* tell me what we're going to spend time on.

And the topic will be wet cement, whatever it is—future integrated converged devices, data analytics in the command center, sensors-based Internet of Things and what it means for public safety—let's ideate, iterate, and talk!'" In other words, putting heads together instead of PowerPoints.

The change had an immediate and dramatic impact on Brown as well as the meetings. "I tried to speak less and speak last," he says. "I didn't want my presence to intimidate anyone, because as soon as I speak first and frame my current thinking, whether it's right or wrong, people feel they need to work around my thesis, maybe even to defer to it. I don't want them to do that. So I go out of my way to ask questions." And shut up more, listen more, and give up a little authority to liberate other people's thinking.

That shift goes hand in hand with a major realignment inside Motorola Solutions. For nearly two decades its venture capital arm reported up to its finance division. Impressed by Silver Lake, as well as by the entrepreneurs he was partnering with, Brown decided to shift venture investments to the technology group, run by Paul Steinberg—a highly unusual move at the time.

"We realized we weren't really converting on these investments. We were making money, which was nice, but that wasn't the point," recalls Steinberg. "We decided we needed to hook it to innovation." Which is why Brown decided to combine the tech division with the ventures capital group under Conrado. "That's so we can share best practices and insights and coalesce that around what they mean for us," he says.

Brown, too, is changing his role. He still oversees financial and operational aspects of the business. But now, he says, "I spend the majority of my time around people, talent development, and talent acquisition—that's category one. And category two is M&A, high-level strategy." These activities push him outside his office a lot. Once he focused on the company's top twenty-five executives. Today he's expanded that radius four-fold. "I know them intimately better," he says. "I meet with all of them personally a few times a year. They all have my cell phone number." And they often shoot him emails and texts.

That's how Brown finds and curries new talent, the source of tomorrow's leaders.

## APPROACH EVERY NEW CHALLENGE AS AN OUTSIDER

As I reflect back on these remarkable leaders—each of them in different ways renegades, outsiders on the inside—I'm reminded of some of the unorthodox things I did during my quarter century at Procter & Gamble.

Nearly a decade after leaving the company, one of the things I'm still remembered for is taking an entourage to the Cannes Lions International Festival of Creativity in 2003. It was the first time a client crashed the party of creative advertising types who flocked to the annual event in southern France, a rowdy bacchanalia and hardly a scene for staid Cincinnatians.

The original idea to invite ourselves came from an outsider, Bob Isherwood, a quiet, introverted Australian who was the creative head at Saatchi & Saatchi, one of P&G's top ad agencies. He said if I wanted P&G to jump-start its creativity, I should go experience the most creative work and creative people in the world. We did—and P&G changed its creative standards forever.

Today, there's still plenty of Bacchus to be found in Cannes, and now one in three delegates are from brand, technology, or media companies. It's become a pretty big deal.

Whatever job I had at P&G, I seemed to do it a little differently from my predecessors. Perhaps that was because whenever I got a new title, I wanted to learn more about the business from the people who worked in different functions—and not just from direct reports. So I'd visit engineers in technical packaging, plant managers, outside suppliers, even farmers when I served in the food division. Not exactly the stuff of marketing poohbahs.

In 1993, as a marketing director, I was sent to Baltimore to work on P&G's newly acquired cosmetic businesses, including the Cover Girl brand—and was about as unwelcome a guest as you can imagine. But instead of overwhelming them with P&G best practices, standard operating procedures at the time, I won them over by asking questions about their best days, their heroes, their feelings about the brand. I used their answers to create the case for change, nudging them back into things like product- and demo-driven ads that had once resonated so well with consumers. I arrived as an outsider, but used some of the experience I'd gained from insiders at P&G to push innovations.

That same approach worked well when I was sent to Prague as general manager of the Czech/Slovak Republics. This wasn't long after the fall of the Berlin Wall and the crumbling of Soviet influence in Eastern Europe in the early 1990s. As a foreigner, I tried to instill something of a P&G culture—mutual respect, high-performance teams, a sense of ownership—in a place where jealousy was rampant and people did not share common goals. One idea I borrowed from P&G practices in other countries: stock options to help unite our teams and share in P&G's long-term success.

I became global marketing officer in 2001, the first person in the chair who had come "from the field," from Baltimore, Prague, Frankfurt, and Geneva. Immediately I broke precedent by drawing my team from key leaders in the major business units and regions—not by creating a group of central staffers. That would have insulated me too much. I wanted exposure to all line businesses and to geographic diversity.

Just as critically, I wanted everyone to own a piece of any success that I achieved or challenges I was struggling with. To underscore the sincerity of that effort, I even shared my performance review from A.G. Lafley with the team—a bit unconventional, but effective in underscoring our shared responsibility.

During the research for this book, I was reminded of the part I played in P&G's very early partnership with Facebook while I was global marketing officer. A lot of those days back in 2005 and 2006 came back to me in a long chat with Kevin Colleran, a managing director of Slow Ventures in San Francisco, which invests in early-stage technology companies. Its swelling portfolio includes Pinterest, Birchbox (which delivers bespoke boxes of luxury beauty products once a month to subscribers), and Slack (cloud-based communications for companies and, increasingly, communities).

Kevin started his first company around the time his voice cracked, went to Babson College (which coins entrepreneurs), and was among the first ten Facebook employees, hired by Sean Parker. Now that he's up in his thirties, I can't help but think of him as that fresh-faced kid I met more than a decade ago. He's still brimming with energy and optimism. And he's got a terrifyingly sharp memory.

Facebook was then a social media site just for college students—and a fraction of the size of MySpace. Moreover, as Kevin reminds me, brands and agencies found it difficult to work with Facebook. Because Mark Zuckerberg hated banner ads and popups, Facebook refused to use the standard ad-serving units on a Web page. "Mark believed there was a much better way to integrate brands within the content in a much more natural way," Kevin recalls. That meant a *lot* of extra work for clients, many of whom thought it wasn't worth the effort.

Then there was the hassle of having to create landing pages because ads on Facebook, as Kevin points out, didn't take you to, say, a Tide.com site, but to a Facebook.com/tide page, and that required a lot of work for a company like P&G.

Zuckerberg insisted that brands and agencies had to design all these units and pages themselves because he couldn't spare the engineering talent to build the tools. You couldn't track ad performance, either, so you never knew if you were targeting the right audience, much less how people were responding to the ad. And, scariest of all, no one could control the Facebook fan pages that were cropping up by the thousands. What if online mobs started trashing your brands?

You have to wonder why anyone went to all the trouble and expense for a tiny company that focused all its efforts on eighteen-to-twenty-two-year-olds. What did that crowd care about brands like Tide and Pampers? Far easier to tick off the social media box with a safer and more accommodating site like MySpace.

I guess I saw something in that fiercely creative little upstart. Kevin had approached me after I gave a keynote at a 2005 conference put on by the Association of National Advertisers and told me all about Facebook. My kids, who were in high school back then, sure felt its power. And so did some forward-thinking P&G marketing leaders: Lucas Watson, who was Kevin Colleran's go-to guy and now is chief marketing and sales officer at Intuit; Stan Joosten, who headed up digital marketing technology; Vivienne Bechtold, who led capability-building in global corporate marketing; and Ted McConnell, a pioneer in interactive marketing who today has his own consultancy.

"P&G is the single most important contribution that I made to Facebook," Colleran recalls. "It's the thing that Sheryl [Sandberg] and Mark still recognize me for." But it was key insiders at Procter—all outward-facing people—who made that happen.

As Kevin points out, they were mostly brand managers who had just graduated from business school or college and who took a big chance betting on Facebook in 2005–6.

"It's tough to take a stand on something so unproven and so new just because you believe in the product so much yourself, because you're such an aggressive user and you know your friends in your age group are—and still knowing that your organization isn't built to either do it or to recognize it or to appreciate it or understand it," muses Kevin.

I suppose that's as good a definition of corporate courage as I've come across in a long time. It takes the exceptional leader to see what isn't there yet—and to take bold action where the endgame, to say nothing of the risks along the way, is unknown. That's the kind of leadership it takes to work through successful partnerships with startups and to carry the best outcomes of those relationships back into the company, where the real work of change and renewal has to begin.

That's the challenge of every legacy enterprise.

# 11

# Are You Ready to Roll?

You rarely win, but sometimes you do.

—ATTICUS FINCH, *in Harper Lee's* To Kill a Mockingbird

So, NOW WHAT? IF YOU HAVE GOTTEN THIS FAR, YOU PROB-ably suspect that your company is in some kind of peril and *has* to change to keep growing. I hope I've convinced you that partnerships with startups can be a great way to ignite those changes—to shake up the old order and bring renewal to your company's sense of purpose and the processes that spark innovation. As we've seen, that approach is certainly starting to produce tangible dividends at proud, established organizations that, just a handful of years ago, seemed to be getting a bit long in the tooth.

What should you do to get started? How can you take the stories and lessons of other companies and apply them to your own?

First, let's review the key questions I've tried to raise throughout the book, which roughly tracks with the chapter flow:

1. *How bad is our situation?* Too many legacy enterprises are endangered. They're hamstrung by their own history of success; threatened on all fronts by younger competitors but entrenched in their way of doing things; slow to

embrace new ideas and terrified of taking risks; cognizant of their shortcomings but paralyzed by fear of change

Sitting down with exciting young companies provides a way out of their troubles. Not only can startups help with specific challenges such as technology advancements, declining revenue, or poor customer engagement, but they can also help energize an existing organization, acting as a catalyst for new ways of thinking and acting. I believe that partnerships, rather than acquisitions, are a better way to achieve all these ends.

2. *Why partner with a startup?* What is the motivation behind partnering with a startup (or several)? The evidence suggests that effective partnering with a startup has a dramatic impact: it delivers lasting benefits in terms of achieving your strategic purpose, solving practical problems, and kicking off a transformation from within.

3. *How do companies discover good candidates?* Finding a good partner, and settling on the goal for that relationship, is the result of loose and tight intention. That is, it helps to have some procedures in place, including a search committee, a small group of insiders who are dedicated to the creation and maintenance of partnerships, or an entrepreneurs-in-residence program. But some of the best matches happen in a much less systematic way—via networking with technology and venture capital organizations, attending conferences and trade shows, getting out and meeting people (and rivals) on a regular basis.

4. *How do companies handle a startup partner?* If you've convinced a startup company to participate in a joint enterprise with your company, you've probably sold it on the advan-

tages you can offer: prominent name, strong manufacturing and supply chains, broad customer base, rich resources, expertise, and so on. Once a partnership has been agreed on, don't hamstring the startup with all kinds of covenants and financial goals.

In fact, I would suggest that you offer the startup more freedom than it may have expected, and put it in charge of key decisions. That doesn't mean ignoring the relationship; it still has to be managed, but in a noncoercive way. You should have the right to veto—but use that power only in extremis. And if things turn sour, you must be able to end things as cleanly as possible. But if you've picked the right people, and if you trust your partner and offer enough autonomy and support, I believe you can help ensure a success you'll both profit from.

5. *How should we manage the initial phase of the partnership?* Having benchmarks is certainly useful. But getting to know each other may be even more critical. Learning something about each other's work habits and cultures, as well as different perspectives and objectives, can help keep long-term goals aligned as the relationship moves forward. While it's easy for one side of the partnership to get ahead of (or fall behind) the other, frequent discussions can keep everyone apprised and help with accommodations and adjustments.

6. *What happens when things veer off course?* Expect that they will. Nothing ever goes as planned, even partnerships that have to meet small, specific milestones. You always have to be prepared to revisit decisions small and large. Good communication, of course, is everything, helping to minimize the worst surprises.

But projects always take longer and require more money

than anyone likes to admit at the start; clear promises made at the beginning have a way of becoming theoretical and increasingly dependent on unforeseen circumstances as the days pass. If the partnership is worth salvaging, be prepared to recalibrate expectations or make changes to get things back on track. If you're too inflexible when things start to fall apart, the center certainly won't hold.

7. *Suppose we fail?* This may be the scariest question of all. Failure is inevitable in at least some of your efforts. That's no reason to shrink from trying something novel or heroic. The best way to defeat your hesitation about risk is to fail often. The more you venture—the greater the number of small bets on partnerships—the lower the cost of failure and the better chance you have of succeeding somewhere in something. And it's important to try to learn from the mistakes, to carry forward a key new lesson that will make you better, stronger, smarter, and more determined the next time you try.

8. *How can leaders light a fire inside the company?* The best kind of kindling is a good outcome from a successful partnership. Inciting change, helping it spread throughout an organization, is a prodigiously difficult effort, even with the blessing of the highest levels. Fear of change is a close cousin to fear of failure.

Many people in every organization have a huge stake in the status quo—even if it's slowly choking the company. So you have to win folks over by persuasion and proof. If you can show people that a new approach works, makes their lives better, is good for the company as a whole, you can gradually turn them from doubters to disciples. But it takes constant, repeatable, uphill effort to do so. Some people are intractable, no matter what. At some point, you may have to confront them with a stark ultimatum.

9. *What does it mean to lead in this new era of partnerships and corporate rejuvenation?* First, it means embracing outsiders—startup partners, industry leaders, other experts in areas of interest who can be helpful, even competitors—as the source of fresh answers to lingering problems and challenges. Inviting these outliers into your company shouldn't be viewed as an intrusion or threat as much as an opportunity to learn from their examples.

But that's just the start. You'll also have to help people inside your organization recognize that they don't have all the solutions to what's ailing the company—that they need to fling open the doors and get out into the world more. This sort of leadership requires humility, experimentation, and coalition building because no one person or powerful team can do this kind of work alone. Renewal on this scale takes years.

How prepared—and willing—is your company, and are you, to jump in? To give you some idea, I've put together a ten-question quiz based on what executives and entrepreneurs have been telling me over the last several years, and on the global quantitative study of partnerships conducted by OgilvyRED.

## UNLEASHING THE INNOVATORS: COMPANY ASSESSMENT

| | YES | NO |
|---|---|---|
| I. Does your company have a compelling purpose? Are employees motivated to achieve your strategic goals and objectives? | | |
| 2. Do you have a clear and compelling reason to partner with a startup? Is it tied to your company's purpose? | | |
| 3. Have you created discrete, multiple goals you will try to achieve in a partnership program? | | |
| 4. Has your company created an internal team to oversee partnerships and hold them accountable for their results? | | |
| 5. Do you have support from the top? Is your team incentivized with the right resources and rewards to make this partnership successful? | | |
| 6. Are people in your company actively and deliberately networking to find potential partners? Do they have particular traits they are screening for? | | |
| 7. Is your company prepared to give startup partners decision-making authority, and enough autonomy to remain in their element as agile, fast-moving risk-takers? | | |
| 8. Are you prepared to fail with half or more of your partnerships—and to reward employees for bold, if unsuccessful, efforts? | | |
| 9. Do you expect your partnerships to have a significant impact in changing the way your company works and what it values? Are you willing to help drive these new changes? | | |

10. Are your key leaders—including the CEO—open to different ideas and approaches from outsiders (startups, strategic partners, competitors)?

| SCORE | ACTION |
| --- | --- |
| 8–10 Yes answers | Buy more of your stock! |
| 6–7  Yes answers | Do even more partnerships. |
| 4–5  Yes answers | Pick 1–2 areas to improve this year. |
| 2–3  Yes answers | Consider hiring a few of the stars in this book. |
| 0–1  Yes answers | Buy this book for everyone in your company! |

Your answers should give you a pretty good snapshot of how things stand within your organization, pinpointing its ability and eagerness to move forward with partnerships—and where it needs strengthening and encouragement. If you and your company notched a high score, congrats: you're probably ready to move ahead and have enough support to sustain that long-term effort. A low rating shouldn't be dispiriting; it means you probably have a lot of missionary work ahead of you. Then again, easy stuff doesn't create heroes.

Now for the tough question: are *you* up for the challenge? As we've learned throughout these chapters, most legacy companies are smart enough to recognize the predicaments they're in. Many of them have a good sense of what they need to do in order to dig themselves out. But, for many of the same reasons they got into trouble, they can't: crippling processes, major investments in the status quo, fear of failure and change. Who or what can break the logjam?

Possibly someone like you. If you've been curious enough to read this book, you're exactly the right kind of person to launch something at your company. Now, that's great if you're a CEO or a senior executive. Set a course and people will follow you. But the role of champion isn't exclusive to the C-suite. You can spark initiatives if you're the head of a business unit, a midlevel manager, or just someone who ultimately aspires to a leadership role. All it takes is imagination—and some courage and grit.

Why is courage important? The question of courage has come up again and again in so many of the interviews I've conducted, through striking examples of corporate audacity—or the lack of it when daring action was called for.

Courage is rarely a pure and unadulterated trait. And, honestly, none of us knows just how much courage and grit we really have until we get into the thick of it. Like a lot of inspiration, courage starts with an idea and calls for a lot of determination to keep going.

One of the most beautiful expressions of courage I've ever encountered comes not from military heroism or corporate derring-do but from the novel *To Kill a Mockingbird*, that timeless coming-of-age story set in a small Alabama town torn by deep racial hatred and violence.

Lawyer Atticus Finch is explaining to his son, Jem, why Mrs. Dubose, a difficult old woman who has shown little but meanness to those she comes in contact with, and who has particularly tormented Jem, has died a hero: racked by pain, she nevertheless decided during her last months to battle and overcome her morphine addiction. "I wanted you to see something about her—I wanted you to see what real courage is, instead of getting the idea that courage is a man with a gun in his hand," Atticus says. "It's when you know you're licked before you begin but you begin anyway and you see it through no matter what. You rarely win, but sometimes you do."

That's a fair rallying cry for this book. Recognizing your own shortcomings—your private ones as well as the weaknesses of your company—can be a source of strength. Reaching out to others, particularly young startups, for answers and then working unremittingly to sign up recruits for change within your organization—that's where the real power of change lies. This is crucial but hard work, punctuated by setbacks, usually inching forward with small victories. Breakthroughs are rare; failures seem to accumulate every day. That's how real progress happens.

The effort has to start somewhere. Why not have it begin with you?

# APPENDIX: THE GLOBAL PARTNERSHIP STUDY

In order to provide a rigorous underpinning to my book and give added power to its conclusions, I commissioned a bespoke quantitative research study to uncover data-driven learnings and insights. This was a first-of-its-kind, global survey of established companies and startups, and was conducted in the second half of 2016.

## WHO WE SURVEYED

A total of 201 decision-makers were surveyed, split among established companies and startups. The surveys were all conducted by phone. In addition, selected respondents were re-contacted for a follow-up discussion, which provided additional insights for the book.

The majority of the established companies in the survey were more than one hundred years old and large and global in scale (annual revenues of $5 billion to more than $100 billion), and all were actively involved in partnerships with startups. The survey covered senior executives in a variety of roles such as strategy, business development, innovation, product development, and operations. Most were C-suite executives, EVPs, SVPs, and VPs, and represented a wide range of industries, including manufacturing, healthcare, transportation, financial services, consumer packaged goods, technology, energy, and many more.

Startup companies in the survey were very young (the

majority were less than five years old) and in various stages of funding (founder, seed, Series A–D), and all were engaged in partnerships with established companies. The participants were owners, CEOs, or business development and strategy executives. The startups represented a variety of industries, including technology, media, financial services, healthcare, consumer packaged goods, manufacturing, and several others. More than a third of the startups were based outside the United States.

## WHAT WE ASKED

We tailored the study to busy senior executives and entrepreneurs who might have little patience and time to deal with a traditional quantitative survey. As such, the questionnaire was carefully designed to be thought-provoking and engaging, sprinkling in conversational elements along with rating-type questions.

For established companies, the questions explored different stages in the development of a collaboration with a startup, including the initial realization, the plan, the partnership, the final outcomes, and beyond: What brings mature companies to the realization that they need help from startups? How do mature companies find startups to partner with? How are partnerships structured? What is the experience of managing the partnerships? What is the longer-term ambition for these partnerships? In what ways were they successful or unsuccessful? How did mature companies change as a result?

For startups, the survey probed the motivations for entering into a partnership with a legacy company, the experience of being in that collaboration, and its impacts. What motivates startups to want to partner with mature companies? What are the rewards and frustrations of the partnerships? What outcomes were achieved? What lasting impact did the partnership have on the startups?

## WHAT WE LEARNED

The survey revealed the counterintuitive idea that partnerships end up being less about technology than about company culture. While established companies tend to enter into partnerships with startups with the goal of acquiring new technology and innovation, many come to realize that successful relationships yield other, sometimes quite different, benefits. The most successful partnerships help to galvanize large and lasting change within the organization.

## HOW COMPANIES APPROACH PARTNERSHIPS

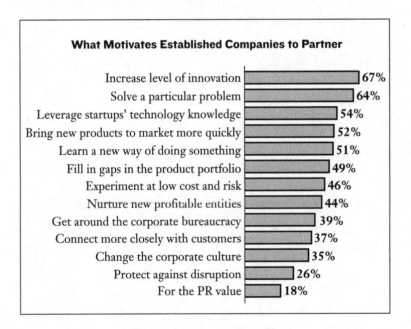

**What Motivates Established Companies to Partner**

| | |
|---|---|
| Increase level of innovation | 67% |
| Solve a particular problem | 64% |
| Leverage startups' technology knowledge | 54% |
| Bring new products to market more quickly | 52% |
| Learn a new way of doing something | 51% |
| Fill in gaps in the product portfolio | 49% |
| Experiment at low cost and risk | 46% |
| Nurture new profitable entities | 44% |
| Get around the corporate bureaucracy | 39% |
| Connect more closely with customers | 37% |
| Change the corporate culture | 35% |
| Protect against disruption | 26% |
| For the PR value | 18% |

The majority of mature companies are initially motivated to partner with startups to improve upon or obtain new technology. Two-thirds (67 percent) want to increase their level of innovation, and more than half (54 percent) want to leverage the startups' technology knowledge. By contrast, only 35 percent are motivated by the opportunity to change their corporate culture to make it more entrepreneurial and risk-taking.

As might be expected, then, the top criterion for vetting potential startup partners is technology match. Mature companies are far more likely to evaluate startups on this basis (63 percent) than on more intangible factors, such as the startup's culture (41 percent) or leadership qualities (37 percent).

The structure of the partnerships also reflects the desire of established companies to extract primarily technological advantages, not broader organizational ones, from the startups. More than half (55 percent) of the legacy companies we surveyed have kept partnerships completely separate from their organization, while only a quarter (26 percent) have included them within a division of their company. Mature companies are also three times more likely to entrust the partnership to a leader from their own company, rather than to one from the startup—a decision that doesn't necessarily correlate with success, as we discovered in follow-up interviews.

**Startups' Motivation to Partner**

| | |
|---|---|
| Access to resources | 23% |
| Get funding | 21% |
| Drive sales/revenue | 20% |
| Access to customers & markets | 15% |
| Access to distribution | 13% |
| Gain scale | 12% |
| Gain credibility | 11% |
| Raise profile | 10% |
| Access technology | 10% |
| Leverage marketing skills | 7% |
| Longer-term sale in mind | 2% |

Startup companies, too, enter into partnerships with a focused set of objectives. Their goals are usually fairly tangible, such as gaining access to resources (23 percent), obtaining funding (21 percent), driving sales (20 percent) or getting entry to new customers or markets (15 percent).

Established companies tend to engage in partnerships with a "we know better" attitude. They are inclined to blame the startups when expectations are not being met. "A startup will tell you they will deliver by a certain time, then it takes longer and things happen along the way," lamented an executive in a financial services company. Legacy companies tend to believe that a startup needs to adjust to *their* ways of doing things. "We had to get the startup knowledgeable about our company and the way that things are done," a retail executive explained. "We have certain processes and business models we need to stick to," said a VP in the consumer packaged goods industry.

Not surprisingly, startup companies, for their part, are frustrated by working with the established companies. While

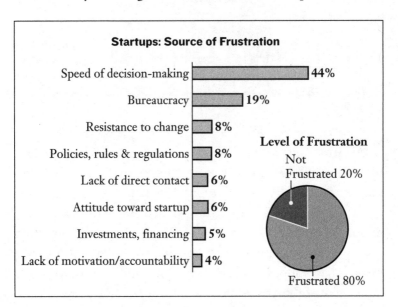

**Startups: Source of Frustration**

| | |
|---|---|
| Speed of decision-making | **44%** |
| Bureaucracy | **19%** |
| Resistance to change | **8%** |
| Policies, rules & regulations | **8%** |
| Lack of direct contact | **6%** |
| Attitude toward startup | **6%** |
| Investments, financing | **5%** |
| Lack of motivation/accountability | **4%** |

**Level of Frustration**

Not Frustrated 20%

Frustrated 80%

the overall mood is positive (91 percent of startups claim that the partnership experience has been positive), a vast majority (80 percent) nevertheless find some cause for frustration. These concerns are usually linked to the larger company's slowness (44 percent), bureaucracy (19 percent), and resistance to change (8 percent).

A majority of established companies said that they met expectations, but defined them in a narrow and discrete way. Almost nine out of ten feel they have been able to solve the particular problem they were tackling, and 85 percent say they have been able to apply a specific new technology or introduce a new product.

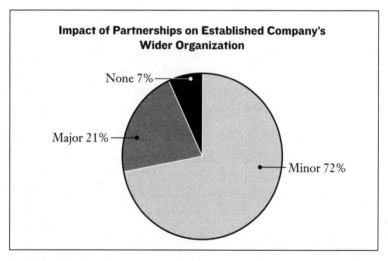

**Impact of Partnerships on Established Company's Wider Organization**

None 7%

Major 21%

Minor 72%

A narrow purpose and rigid attitude ensure that partnerships by most established companies are unlikely to have a major impact on their wider organization. About three-quarters of the mature companies say that the partnerships have had only a minor impact on their organization. Only 21 percent have been successful in extracting broad organization-wide impacts from their collaborations with startups—the ultimate outcome of most successful partnerships.

## WHAT ACTUALLY WORKS

**Partnerships' Success Rate by Motivation Reason (For Established Companies)**

| Motivation Reason | Success Rate |
| --- | --- |
| Connect more closely with customers | 70% |
| Change the corporate culture | 67% |
| Leverage startups' technology knowledge | 67% |
| Learn a new way of doing something | 65% |
| Get around the corporate bureaucracy | 65% |
| Fill in gaps in the product portfolio | 65% |
| Bring new products to market more quickly | 63% |
| Solve a particular problem | 61% |
| Increase level of innovation | 53% |
| Nurture new profitable entities | 52% |
| Protect against disruption | 45% |
| For the PR value | 40% |
| Experiment at low cost and risk | 40% |

Mature companies are more likely to be successful when they adopt a broader outlook entering into partnerships. When established companies are driven purely by innovation, the success rate of their partnerships is about even (53 percent). On the other hand, when the motivation is to change their corporate culture or to connect more closely with customers, the success rate of partnerships rises (67 percent and 70 percent, respectively). Further, mature companies would do well to beware of sheer vanity projects—when the motivation is to gain PR value, the success rate is low (40 percent).

Established companies are also more likely to be successful when they structure their partnerships to embrace change rather than to isolate its impacts. Partnerships are almost twice as likely (1.7x) to have a major impact on the wider organization when they are within a division of the larger company rather than being kept completely separate. And when established companies entrust the decision-making to a leader from the startup, their partnerships are more successful than when they install someone from their own organization (75 percent vs. 62 percent success rate).

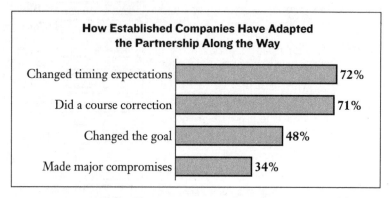

**How Established Companies Have Adapted the Partnership Along the Way**

| | |
|---|---|
| Changed timing expectations | 72% |
| Did a course correction | 71% |
| Changed the goal | 48% |
| Made major compromises | 34% |

A majority of established companies learn to be flexible along the way. Most have adjusted their expectations about timing (72 percent) or performed mid-course corrections (71 percent), while some have made more drastic changes, such as changing goals (48 percent) or making major compromises (34 percent).

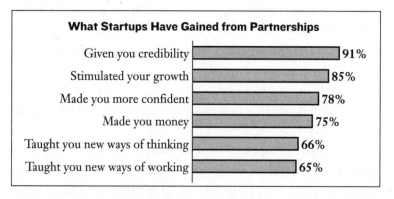

**What Startups Have Gained from Partnerships**

| | |
|---|---|
| Given you credibility | 91% |
| Stimulated your growth | 85% |
| Made you more confident | 78% |
| Made you money | 75% |
| Taught you new ways of thinking | 66% |
| Taught you new ways of working | 65% |

Startups, too, can discover surprising benefits from such collaborations. The partnerships often deliver expected pluses, such as stimulating growth (85 percent) or making money (75 percent), but they also help them in intangible, more far-reaching ways, such as giving them credibility (91 percent) and teaching them new ways of thinking and working (65-66 percent).

## THE REWARDS OF A SUCCESSFUL PARTNERSHIP

When legacy companies take a more enlightened stance toward their partnerships, approaching them with broader motivations and a welcoming embrace of any ensuing changes, the rewards can be far-reaching. Successful partnerships are nearly three times (2.8x) more likely to have a major favorable impact on a large organization than unsuccessful ones.

Executives from such established companies recognize that they have reaped far greater rewards beyond their original goals. "Without some of the startup partnerships we have had, we wouldn't have been in business or grown," claimed a VP in the manufacturing sector. A media and entertainment executive thoughtfully said, "The partnership moved us closer to the consumer by challenging our heavy corporate culture. We weren't prepared for that, we had to change our outlook."

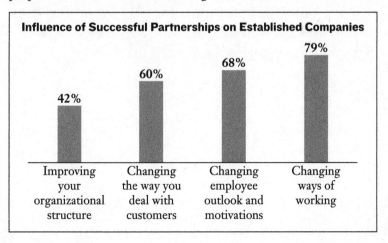

Influence of Successful Partnerships on Established Companies

| Improving your organizational structure | Changing the way you deal with customers | Changing employee outlook and motivations | Changing ways of working |
|---|---|---|---|
| 42% | 60% | 68% | 79% |

Beyond appreciating the immediate benefits of successful partnerships, a majority of companies have found themselves changing the way they work (79 percent), their outlook (68 percent), the way they deal with customers (60 percent), and even their organizational structure (42 percent). Legacy companies with successful partnerships have introduced measures to instill a startup mentality in their wider organization, such as new benefits, moving to a new location, incentivizing innovation, and changing office configurations.

Established companies define success as not just about driving the partnership to the finish line but also exploiting the gains as a way to rejuvenate the entire company. "The startups challenged our thinking and how we view ourselves. Sure it is painful and it hurts a little, but you have to transform in order to learn, grow, and be successful," declared a media executive. An executive in manufacturing revealed, "We plan to use the startup's creative nature to spark excitement within our company."

For startups, success can be defined as a win for both parties. "The partnership has led to an increase in business for both parties," said an executive in manufacturing. Despite all the frustrations, more than three-fourths of startups have decided not only to continue their existing partnership but to ramp it up. And the future of such collaborations looks bright—78 percent of startups plan to do it again.

# ACKNOWLEDGMENTS

Live and learn.

That old hackneyed phrase has almost always had negative overtones, suggesting regret ("I should have invested in Facebook when the stock was $18! Well, live and learn").

But I mean it in a strictly positive sense. The concept of living and learning sums up the major themes of this book and describes how its central idea evolved.

Some books take awhile to unfold. This one started with a discussion in late 2014 with my literary agent, Richard Pine of Inkwell Management, who was also so helpful in my first book, *Grow*. We talked about all the brash young startups that seemed so self-confident, perhaps dangerously so. Couldn't older, more established companies teach them a thing or two? Further conversation refined that theme: maybe young companies also help revitalize mature enterprises struggling to grow their top line sales. The more I started talking to big and small businesses, the more convinced I was that they could come to one another's aid. And the main vehicle for this kind of exchange turned out to be partnerships between them.

Richard was helpful in another way: he introduced me to my collaborator and co-author, Tom Post. From the beginning, Tom and I agreed on a key principle: we wanted to write a helpful business book that was actually enjoyable to read. Tom and I traveled thousands of miles together, interviewed dozens of leaders, and every Monday for almost two years did a mind melt on the emerging ideas in this book. Tom was deeply committed from the start; I cannot thank him enough for his curiosity about the human stories behind these partnerships, his collaborative spirit, his lively prose, and the friendship we developed in the journey of this book.

Another key turning point in the development of the book came months later from Roger Scholl, my gifted and generous editor at Crown. "Make up your mind," Roger counseled at our first meeting, "and focus your attention on either the young pups or the big guys—not both." Unhesitatingly, we chose large corporations as our main audience. They had the resources to invest in partnerships and, in some ways, the most to learn. And speaking of resources, a huge shout of gratitude to Crown Publisher Tina Constable, who has been so supportive in all my literary efforts, and to Megan Schumann and Megan Perritt, who handle the company's public relations and marketing.

My team in Cincinnati simply amazes me every day. They found a way to get this book done while running a thriving consulting and leadership-training operation. Liz Keating, our company's marketing director, was the eternally optimistic and persistent captain of the book, connecting with dozens of large companies and startups, and helping to extract the learning that makes this book so helpful to others. Liz also was the critical liaison with Crown's smart and creative marketing team. Betty Gabbard, our calm and committed business manager and my longtime P&G associate, was indispensable in her counsel, editing, and impeccable coordination of countless moving parts. Sue Whitehouse, my ever-smiling, indefatigable executive assistant, made all the scheduling, appointments, communication, and follow-up happen on top of a growing, dynamic workload. Renée Dunn and Matt Carcieri, two of our senior growth consultants, read the early manuscript and gave me blunt and invaluable input to make this more useful for leaders in legacy companies. Thank you, Liz, Betty, Sue, Renée, and Matt—I am fortunate to be in your company every day.

Early in our journey, when I decided we needed a quantitative underpinning to our large qualitative database, I reached out to Joanna Seddon, president of global brand consulting at Ogilvy-RED. I have worked with Joanna for fifteen years, and she is a superb advisor and researcher. Joanna, Nikhil Gharekhan, Julia Hawley, and the team at OgilvyRED designed and delivered the first-ever global study of partnerships between established companies and startups; the insights from that study—and their counsel—have given the learning in this book more gravitas.

OVER THE COURSE of two years and more while researching the book, I came to realize just how much leaders of older companies were grappling with during their mighty efforts to stay relevant, master new technologies and lessons, and rejuvenate themselves—exhausting but heroic efforts. Reconnecting with some of the executives I've known, worked with, and served on boards with, I came to appreciate in a new light what their challenges are, and the earnest and creative ways they're trying to overcome them.

This project also put me in touch with remarkable leaders I'd never met before. To all of them I owe deep appreciation for their willingness to open their doors and tell their stories in frank and unvarnished ways that demonstrate how hard and humbling the process of change can be. And I'm grateful for their generosity in devoting their time and introducing me to their colleagues who are helping to revive their companies' purpose.

I've known Beth Comstock, who is vice chair of GE and

oversees its Business Innovations, for years, back when she was GE's first CMO and working on Ecomagination—bringing environmental products and sensibilities to industrial clients. Beth opened me to the world of GE's FastWorks, a mighty push to reinvent the company, and some of its most ardent architects and practitioners—Viv Goldstein, global director of innovation acceleration and cofounder of FastWorks; Janice Semper, leader, GE Culture; Sue Siegel, CEO of GE Ventures and healthymagination; and Aarif Aziz, head of GE's HR in India—as well as partners like Evidation Health's Deborah Kilpatrick and Bionic's David Kidder.

Another old friend from my days at Procter & Gamble is Jon Iwata. As the senior VP of marketing and communications at IBM, Jon played a behind-the-scenes but indispensable part in the book by exposing me to amazing things going on inside Big Blue and at collaborators like Box CEO Aaron Levie. Through Jon I met leading evangelists of Watson, IBM's truly astonishing artificial intelligence platform: CMO Stephen Gold, as well as John Phelan and Sarah Plantenberg of the Bluemix Garage in San Francisco. And I came into contact with such partners as Don White of Satisfi Labs and Connectidy's Arthur Tisi, who are pushing IBM into places it has never ventured into before.

Greg Brown and Eduardo Conrado (respectively, Motorola Solutions' CEO and chief innovation and strategy officer) are folks I've known for more than a decade. We got acquainted while I served on Motorola's board as it contended with shareholder activists and an epic corporate mitosis into Motorola Solutions and Motorola Mobility. But it wasn't until we visited again that I learned just how far they've pushed the old walkie-talkie company into sci-fi territory when it comes to life-saving technologies for fire, emergency, and police officers. CTO Paul Steinberg, venture capital honcho Reese Schroeder, and senior strategy manager Sean Taylor fleshed out the challenges and rewards of working with cutting-edge partners.

My friend and former P&G colleague Chip Bergh is known at Levi Strauss & Co., where he's now CEO, for pushing an aggressively pro-growth agenda—and for never washing his jeans. He also threw open Levi's Eureka Labs to us, sharing some of its most daring experiments with fashion and fabric, particularly its partnership with Google to produce a "smart" denim jacket. Leading that effort are a passionate duo—Bart Sights, senior director of technical innovation, and Paul Dillinger, the head of global product innovation—who spent hours taking me and my team through this significant collaboration.

P&G alum Will Papa helped me appreciate how big companies recover from failure by detailing the new frontiers that The Hershey Co., where he is now the chief R&D officer, is pushing into. Rick Dalzell, whom I got to know when we both served on the AOL board, taught me much about taking risks in recalling his decades at Walmart and Amazon. And Kevin Colleran, a managing director of the investment firm Slow Ventures, helped me relive early collaborations between P&G and Facebook, where he was one of Mark Zuckerberg's earliest hires.

Tim Armstrong (CEO of Oath), John Haugen (VP and general manager at 301 INC, General Mills's venture arm), and Zack Hicks (CIO of Toyota Motor North America) also helped with this book. While their individual stories have little in common, they do share one important characteristic: they are all indefatigable promoters of change within large organizations, and they're unashamed to reach far outside their companies for help along the way.

The stirrings of innovation at Wells Fargo, Shire, and Target were all new to me when I started this project. I learned how the bank is pushing a startup accelerator, pairing young companies with division leaders, thanks to efforts by Steve Ellis, an EVP and head of the Innovation Group, and Braden More, head of partnerships and industry relations for Wells Fargo's payments business. At Shire, a drug maker that focuses on rare diseases, CEO Flemming Ørnskov has turned partnerships with startups into the central strategy for growth and reorganization of the entire company. One of the brightest surprises for me was Target and its multipronged approach to rethinking retail. I was able to see its experiments with the Internet of Things (via Gene Han, head of its San Francisco Innovation Center) and to spend time with some of the first graduates of its Techstars Retail, a startup accelerator, including the Moncayo brothers (Inspectorio) and Jackie Ros (Revolar).

This book would never have been written without multiple visits to the other side of the partnership equation—startups. Driven and determinedly focused as all great entrepreneurs must be, these folks nevertheless devoted hours to helping me understand their collaborations with mature companies, the motives, the recalibrations, and the outcomes. Special thanks to Zain Jaffer, founder and CEO of Vungle, whose mission is to make mobile ads fun and relevant through short videos; Toby Rush, founder and CEO of EyeVerify, a biometric and security company; Rick Morrison, cofounder and CEO of Comprehend Systems, an online platform that helps pharmaceutical companies keep track of the myriad data on patient enrollments, clinical trials, and compliance issues; and Alex Hertel, cofounder and CEO of Xperiel, which is enhancing sports fan engagement by turning scoreboards and stadiums into gaming and entertainment centers.

Few of the dozens and dozens of meetings and phone calls could have taken place without the help of public relations folks like Jenna Reck (Target), Kate Dyer (Motorola Solutions), Sasha Houlihan and Kristin Schwarz (GE), and Gabby Gugliocciello, Nancy Ngo, and Erin Lehr (IBM), whose competence and cheerfulness survived multiple requests at odd hours.

I can't end properly without thanking a couple of invaluable counselors whom you won't find in the book. David Hirsch, cofounder and managing partner of Compound, a seed-stage investment firm in New York City, introduced me to several young companies that do figure in these pages. I first met David when he was overseeing Google's vertical markets group; today, I count on his perspicacity and rich acquaintance with the startup scene and have invested in a couple of his portfolio companies. Ron Conway, whose hundreds of early investments include Google, PayPal, Facebook, Pinterest, Square, and BuzzFeed, was generous with his time and insights. Conway, too, led me to some great young entrepreneurs.

David Rose, an angel investor whom you met in Chapter 2, unwittingly helped frame an important starting point. A buoyant cheerleader for startups, Rose is a Cassandra when it comes to corporate America. Early in my gathering process, he filled me with dire scenarios that awaited legacy companies that remained deaf to the clarion call for radical change infused with entrepreneurial spirit. I thought he protested too much. Little did I know then.

Live and learn.

# INDEX

## About the Authors

JIM STENGEL is the former global marketing officer of Procter & Gamble, and he is now founder and CEO of The Jim Stengel Company, a think tank and leadership consultancy focused on purpose-activated growth. A prolific writer, speaker, and advisor to both blue-chip companies and startups, Jim is the author of *Grow: How Ideals Power Growth and Profit at the World's Greatest Companies*, and his thinking is often cited in the *New York Times*, the *Wall Street Journal*, and on CNBC. He was named to Fortune's first Executive Dream Team and is an inductee to the American Marketing Association's Hall of Fame. Jim serves as a Senior Fellow at Northwestern's Kellogg School of Management and is a former member of the board of directors for AOL and Motorola. He and his wife, Kathleen, have two children and split their time between Cincinnati, Ohio, and Coronado, California.

TOM POST is a former managing editor at Forbes Media, where he oversaw stories about legacy companies and entrepreneurs. As a journalist at *Fortune*, *Newsweek*, and ABC's *World News Tonight*, he covered business and foreign affairs. He is currently senior vice president for content at SnappConner PR.

**Ten years of research uncover
the secret source of growth and profit.**

JIM STENGEL

How Ideals
Power Growth
and Profit at the
World's Greatest
Companies

gROW

"A new powerful model for business . . . A must-read . . .
for all business leaders."

—Sheryl Sandberg, *COO, Facebook*

"By combining a scientist's rigor with a storyteller's
gifts, Jim Stengel has produced a brilliant, must-read
book supremely suited to our times."

—Arianna Huffington